"This is an important book for everyone. Brain trauma affects so many, and it's a hidden wound that is misunderstood. Having Melissa's journey available will not only provide an entertaining read, but lessons that will be thought of for a long time."
—Damien Echols

"This book has it all—rock, roll and redemption—with a heavy dose of pop culture and comics. And it all began from a Judas Priest concert. Melissa Meszaros finds her way back to the life she felt born for, and we share in the journey." —Jeff Krulik, *Heavy Metal Parking Lot, Heavy Metal Picnic, Led Zeppelin Played Here*

"HEAVY METAL HEADBANG reminds you, with brutal honesty and dark humor, that if you're going through hell—keep going."
—Lundon Boyd, *Liars, Fires, And Bears; Poor Boy*

"Melissa Meszaros's HEAVY METAL HEADBANG is an intense, intimate memoir of resilience in the face of trauma. If you think you've read anything like it before, you've got another thing comin'." —Andy Burns, *Wrapped in Plastic: Twin Peaks, The Art and Making of The Stand*

"...goes down like butter. I haven't read an autobiography this enjoyable in a long time! Beautiful, wise, electrifying prose."
— Chris Estey, *Best Music Writing, The Believer, How the Homeless Listen to Music*

MELISSA MESZAROS

HEAVY METAL
HEADBANG

Edited by J. Bryan Jones

Oil On Water Press

OIL ON WATER PRESS
First published in 2022
office@oilonwaterpress.com

HEAVY METAL HEADBANG

10 9 8 7 6 5 4 3 2 1

A CIP catalogue record for this book is
available from the British Library

ISBN PAPERBACK   978-1-909394-85-8
ISBN E-BOOK   978-1-909394-86-5
NO-ISBN   HARDBACK

ORIGINAL TRUE-LIFE STORIES & MEMOIR

Exclusive content at OILONWATERPRESS.COM

For Elizabeth

CONTENTS

||||||||||||||||||||||||||||||||||||||||||||||||||

FOREWORD

⁓⁓⁓⁓⁓⁓⁓⁓⁓⁓⁓⁓⁓⁓⁓⁓⁓⁓⁓⁓⁓⁓⁓⁓⁓⁓⁓⁓⁓⁓⁓⁓

I CAN HARDLY call myself a writer. I write but don't write prose for other people. My day job is promoting books and I can't begin to think of writing for myself. I'm a contradiction. A two-faced dichotomy. I hate the term "introverted extrovert" or "ambivert." I'm a sardonic optimist, maybe. Maybe because I hate labels. I see the black and white but all I feel is gray. I don't take sides. I don't like controversy or unwarranted opinions. I'm more comfortable fading into the background. I want to know about everything without being a part of anything, but I'm a team player. I don't care about success, but would measure my own through what I've given others, and will tell you life's not a pissing contest. We're all just pawns, in ways. All the tropes. I learned this by my life being leveled.

Three years ago I suffered a severe traumatic brain injury (TBI). *You know, when a sudden external force caused your brain to shake loose and crash into your skull?* What to me felt uncommon is actually quite common. From athletes to accidents, one-and-a-half to two-million American adults and children suffer one each year. The same goes for getting hit by a car in America. Pedestrian deaths hit a twenty-eight-year high in 2018: an estimated 6,227 pedestrians were killed, an increase of 250 from 2017.

Weird to think I could've been part of that statistic.

Sustaining a TBI or getting hit by a car could happen anywhere and at any time, and it doesn't matter who the fuck you are. In 1970, Keith Moon accidentally killed his driver and bodyguard after the man got caught under Moon's vehicle and was dragged down the road; in 2001, Rebecca Gayheart hit a third-grader with her car and he later died as a result of his injuries; and in 2018, MTV host and veteran radio DJ Matt Pinfield was hospitalized after being hit by a car. He was crossing the street according to the report. In 1988, actor Gary Busey crashed his motorcycle and fractured his skull. The brain damage was permanent.

Man versus machine.

It's evolution, baby...

While accidents make headlines, brain injuries and their aftermath don't, unless you die or have a triumphant recovery story like comedian Tracy Morgan. From bumps and bruises to broken bones and blood clots, the brain is the commander in chief of our entire body. It tells our hearts to beat, delegates motor skills, affixes identity to sensory details, grants emotion and memory. Without brains we're dead. And when it comes to battle wounds to the noggin, well, it's not always "what you see is what you get." Forget preexisting complications for the moment and consider which part (or parts) of the head have been bludgeoned. Forget the phrenology map and take a look at the general anatomy of the brain, each side, lobe, and what its function is. Now imagine *that* being damaged on top of apparent physical damage. Consider how that part of the brain functions. Its wires and nerves. Add a concussion to the mix, or worse off, a coma. Add a lot of time and therapy depending on how long you've been alive, and there you have it! No two brain injuries are ever alike.

I AM A publicist. A comic book publicist to be exact. I promote comic books and those who create them. Even when I tell people this, they still have no clue what I do. So here's the abridged description—

Publicity is giving notice or attention to someone or something by the media. A *publicist*, or *public relations rep*, is a person who handles the professional maintenance of a favorable public image by a company or other organization or a famous person. PR for short. Day-to-day, I do PR. I write press releases and send them to journalists, schedule interviews and appearances, and build as well as maintain relationships with folks in the entertainment industry and entertainment media. I have a refined skillset that is defined by pragmatism, critical thinking, honesty, knowledge and research, creative writing skills, avid multitasking, and extreme adaptation to problem-solving.

This shit ain't easy.

A lot of it is innate.

And what's learned and earned, takes years.

Now consider all of the above: I don't call myself a writer, not really. I write only to promote others. I am a publicist who sustained a traumatic brain injury.

After my TBI, I'd become *tabula rasa*. A blank slate. I had to earn a lot of the above skills back because all that stuck was what was deeply ingrained, and what I had done forever when it all went to shit—I'd write. It became an exercise in memory mapping, which I wrote entirely on Google Docs, on my iPhone, at my leisure, when something sparked. At the time I didn't consider how much I could or would write—the word count adding up—or that it could even be cohesive enough to make a book. I just wanted to get back some memories that had been taken away. I wanted to remember my stories and what made me who I was, how I got there.

Honestly, I found it quite self-deprecating.

The hubris.

Imposter syndrome.

Piquing narcissistic mortification.

This was an out-of-body experience that reminded me of touring Alfred Lunt and Lynn Fontanne's Ten Chimneys estate that was built in 1915. The great theatrical couple turned their plantation into a living theater playset. The location of each structure's placement and windows were strategically sundialed to the Wisconsin summer to emulate a stage limelight. Each room used props, like nails used to fake candlewick in the chandeliers. But most of all Ten Chimneys was used to hide the couple's penchant for polyamory.

Nothing as juicy will be found here perhaps, nor will the use of names; after all, a good publicist never gives away their secrets. Sure, there are also those folks who would like to see the roster of celebrities I've worked with, but that's also quite unprofessional. Get used to me scraping the surface, because for once, it isn't all about them.

But just in case you're wondering, I am *zero* degrees from Kevin Bacon...

"Maybe that's enlightenment enough: to know that there is no final resting place of the mind; no moment of smug clarity. Perhaps wisdom... is realizing how small I am, and unwise, and how far I have yet to go."
Anthony Bourdain

LEGENDARY

IIIIIIIIIIIIIIIIIIIIIIIIIIIIIIIIIIIIIIIIIIIIIIIIIIIIIIIIIII

IN THE BACK of the ambulance, I called Blondie, who I was supposed to meet.

"My head hurts."

"Yeah, you were hit by a car."

It's true. I'd been hit by a car in a crosswalk on my way to see Judas Priest. Whether shock or delirium, it didn't register how or why she knew what happened. I was a block down from where she was waiting for me.

"It's PIZZA WEEK," I said. "And what about JUDAS PRIEST?!"

It was the day we had ceremoniously counted down to. April 17, 2018. Nuanced and haphazardly thematic, just like us. Our time for New York slices and '80s metal. A slight promotion from the typical post-work happy hour.

"I gotta go, my head hurts." Then I hung up.

Strapped to a gurney, my mind trailed off. I felt each bump in the road and blip on the heart monitor as the ambulance sped its way up to the hospital on the southwest hill of Portland to OHSU. Looking up at the medics I pleaded, "Guys, look, I don't need to go to the hospital." My eyes fixated on the ceiling. This would change the whole trajectory of the situation, of my life. The severity of which, I was in no way fully aware.

Seeing Judas Priest was a self-fulfilling fantasy. Sipping on an overpriced plastic cup of Budweiser, belting out the lyrics to "You've Got Another Thing Comin" with a mouthful of squeeze-cheese nachos as Rob Halford drove his Harley onto the stage and we watched from the peanut gallery—Judas Priest was legendary. Always. I felt deep down that it was my destiny to be part of something legendary. Always.

Legendary was the status quo.

It's what kept me out almost every night for most of my twenties. First escaping to Pittsburgh from the cowtown in western Pennsylvania where I grew up, moving to Columbus, Ohio, and from there, across the US to Portland, Oregon. I mostly settled there for over a decade, with brief stints in Reno, Las Vegas, Anchorage, and Los Angeles. All while frequenting San Francisco.

I had yet to give up hope that every time I went out, it was going to be the best night ever.

NODDING OFF HERE and there, I came to, somewhat, in the emergency room. A male nurse stood over me, deciding, scissors in hand, to shear my perfectly fitted *Screaming For Vengeance* t-shirt. The sterility of white light barely alarmed me, but when he insisted on cutting as opposed to me pulling it over my head in case of a neck fracture—

"It's vintage! Don't!" And before I could be stopped, I slipped the shirt up and over my blood-matted platinum hair. "Look, see? Got it. Told you so."

He snapped a neck brace on me. Hooked me to a morphine drip. Suddenly, slipping out of consciousness, my eyes opened to silhouettes of coworkers and colleagues in the comic book industry hovering over me. A comic convention gone awry.

I HAD BEEN an entertainment publicist for several years. First in music, then in film—only to ultimately work my way into a salaried position in comics publishing. I never wanted to attend college, but my parents implored me that if I didn't, I'd go nowhere in life. (I'd like to thank a sandwich shop employee whose mere existence punted me so hard, with her six kids and wife-beater-sporting husband, for the final push to attend college.) So my undergraduate degree, after attending four local universities, was a hodgepodge manifestation, "Interdisciplinary Studies," with a focus in writing and communications to dodge the required Shakespeare courses of a general English Lit degree. I didn't give a fuck about literature back then. I wanted to write and experience a life outside of the one I was born into. A life that started long before I moved to the pacific northwest, to Portland, for my fifth and final attempt at achieving a bachelor's degree—a life that met its rebirth at the tender age of twenty-two.

AUGUST OF 2005, in Columbus, Ohio, I went to see a band embering in the underground psychedelic movement that commercial bands like Oasis left in their wake. It was a sold-out show, but for a college town, that wasn't much to brag about. Equipped with merely a post-teen bravado, I made my way past the monochrome-clad American Apparel hipsters into the dive and noted all major points of interest: the loo, the bar, the stage. I'd graduated from Pabst Blue Ribbon to Newcastle Brown Ale that year, if only to give off an extra bit of cool, which I obviously wasn't; swayback, wearing a waffle shirt and flare jeans from Goodwill, with a red acrylic knit bag slung over my shoulder.

I tried.

The liquor bottles glinted with sinking sunlight that shot through the entryway. Ordering a beer, I made eye contact with an older, lanky man wearing a denim button-down. His dark eyes peered beyond the canopy of his unibrow, beneath the frays of a greasy pudding bowl haircut. He walked up to me. Slouched over the bar. Crossed his wrists, relaxed, the sleeves of his shirt flowered out to his knuckles.

"Got a smoke?" he asked.

Twenty years my senior. I quietly guffawed at his low-rise Jimmy Page fuck-me flares and shiny boots.

"Here," I conceded, pulling a Camel from the square of my pack.

He puffed his chest and grabbed the cigarette. Tipped his head up and asked, "You coming outside, or what?"

I saw no real reason to say no. I'd been reading *The 48 Laws of Power* by Robert Greene, acquired from a friend who was studying to be a lawyer. I figured if I had the knowledge to navigate through the social philosophies, it would have way more impact than shaving my head to stave off unwanted advances.

"You live here?" he asked, leaning back on the building.

I shook my head.

He rolled the cigarette between his thumb and forefinger. "This place sucks."

Not knowing better, I thought Columbus was alright, considering I could freely shop for vintage at Rag-o-Rama. Plus, it had more than one punk bar to choose from.

"It's not *that* bad," I retorted, crouching on the sidewalk in an empty doorway. "Hot as balls, but not bad."

He was silent, in an almost-artistic reverie. Sweat beads morphed from my skin and I pretended not to notice that my bag's red dye began staining the shirt beneath it. A boy with a tiny notepad in hand darted over from the lingering line outside the venue.

"Can I have your autograph, man?" the boy asked. I noticed the tangle of peachy chest hairs poking out from the boy's body as he trembled.

"Dude, I'm having a conversation. *Do you mind?*" he scoffed through a plume of smoke.

The boy slowly turned away cowering, his joy deflated.

The man flashed a broken Chiclet smile at me. "Have any requests to add to the set?"

The Singer. *That's* who the man was.

The moment where my apathy became intrigue.

"I do, in fact."

He sucked his cigarette to the nub and vanished. Walking back inside I was left to wonder if what just happened meant anything. Ladies in tea-dyed lace leaped towards the stage like miniature gazelles. Frat boys hung around the back exit where a low-hanging sign forbade stage diving and moshing. A bass line rang out, amps shook, a high note hummed. The lights went low.

The Singer approached the mic. His voice shook the walls.

"This song's for a sweet little short girl."

THE ESCAPIST

||||||||||||||||||||||||||||||||||||||||||||||||||||||||||||||||||

HOW DID I get hit by a car? Crossing the street to leave work, just as I had every other day. Same spot. Traffic flow was always manageable because every intersection, whether marked or unmarked in the state of Oregon, is a crosswalk. With complete subliminal agility, I always waited in each lane until the subsequent car came to a stop and let me pass. Never was hit before, so what the fuck made this time so different?

Two of my coworkers leaving the building found me lying unconscious on the car-clustered street. They thought I was dead. I hadn't moved for five minutes. Then, magically, I woke up.

As one went to get paper towels for the gash in the back of my head, the other held my hand, "My head hurts," I told her.

"You were hit by a car."

I attempted to further close my leather jacket. "I'm cold."

"You're lying in the street," she said. "The paramedics are coming."

"Why?"

Tears may have welled beyond her wire-rimmed glasses, which I only surmised by the trepidation in her voice. "You have to go to the hospital."

"Can't. I'm going to see Judas Priest."

When the medics arrived they asked me to wiggle my toes. According to my coworker, they sat me up and began the interrogation.

"Where are you?"

"The road."

"What city are we in?"

My response was delayed. "Portland. Duh."

My body was loaded into the ambulance where I saw another coworker's coif blowing beyond a sea of unrecognizable heads. A bald policeman (in what appeared to be a pair of narrow knock-off Oakleys) reached in and handed me his card. No idea what he said to me, then they closed the back doors.

I most likely looked at the paramedic and said, *"I'll take a ride to the hospital, but when I get there, I'm just going to take a Lyft to Judas Priest."*

Persistent because, not only was I unaware, but I also hated missing out on goals. I hate hurdles, missteps, and obstacles—but I flourish in the challenge to make it all right. In some ways, it's almost an obsession to meet perfection to a fault because I grew up in a household of heavy competition. My middle sister, the straight-A student, and oldest sister, the athlete. I was the youngest growing up in a latchkey family, left to my own devices. Reality was never a concept, so creativity took a lovely stranglehold. And my imagination, informed by television, I think, was less than vivid, thanks to pop culture shows.

In my mind the house with the large pillars down the block was the White House transported from D.C., where Mr. Belvedere conveniently lived. Next door to my house, Hawkeye Pierce and Laverne DeFazio were happily married. Smurfs lived under mushrooms, the Jabberwocky hid in the woods, and Chucky ran amok to slice up some unsuspecting victims. I would sit in my bedroom with the door

locked, braiding friendship bracelets I had taped to my boombox, or
drawing portraits of Joey McIntyre while listening to "Please Don't Go
Girl" on a loop. I hoped that one day Joey would appear at my doorstep,
roses in hand, to whisk me away to live with him and the rest of the
New Kids on the Block, because in my mind, they lived together.

For sure it was this hopeful delusion that sucked me into the
vortex known as Entertainment Public Relations, where I could cross
creative fiction with reality with ease and exchange lack of control for
a hint of career navigation via palm pilot as I saw fit.

The city was where it all happened. The older I got, the more I
wanted to escape to revel in the tall buildings, lit skylines, culture.
Even in the 1990s, the run-down steel mill city of Pittsburgh seemed
massive and hopeful. My friends and I would frequent punk shows
at Club Laga, where I learned about 'zine culture and how to properly
wear baggy jeans to compliment tiny kid-sized vintage t-shirts. By the
time I was sixteen, I was traveling to Cleveland for concerts that were
more my taste—from The Odeon in the Flats to Beachland Ballroom
and the Grog Shop in Cleveland Heights. Going to shows in the city
had become a vice that helped me cope with feeling different, the
monotony of living in my hometown, which I heard someone once
refer to as "the land of lady beehive hair and endless hotdog shops."

Western Pennsylvania, in its Silent Generation quaintness, kept
a small-town integrity up until drug dealers started moving in. And,
on a separate note, became a haven for OxyContin which eventually
transpired into heroin addiction for many who resided there. I only
see this in hindsight, however. I moved away long before the decline
of that retro east coast Euro-driven civilization.

I remember the man-made lake across the route from my
neighborhood of 500 residents. Lying awake at night to hear the
thunder of motorcycles rushing to the local bar four blocks away.
The heavy summer rainfall and sliding across the grass as the floods

began to rage—the smell of the warm, wet pavement. The tiger lily fields that bloomed in late summer. Lightning bugs. Kids illegally picking strawberries for three dollars an hour. The childhood home I left back in Pennsylvania is not the place I recognize today, but I can now safely say the same about Portland, Oregon. And myself.

LOCATION, LOCATION

IIIIIIIIIIIIIIIIIIIIIIIIIIIIIIIIIIIIIIIIIIIIIIIIIIIIIIIIIIIIIIIIIIIIIIIIIIIIIIIIIIIIIIIIIIIIIIIIIIIII

I WAS TOO far gone during the initial MRI and CT scan to remember the procedures and tests. No broken ribs or fractured vertebrae as doctors initially thought, despite the crippling pain in my left side that came with impact from the car.

"We have to keep you in the intensive care unit," a faceless man in scrubs said. "You have two skull fractures and a hematoma."

"Hematoma?"

"A bleed between your skull and brain. It's six millimeters. If it gets to ten, you could have permanent brain damage, or you could die."

Die didn't mean a thing.

In a fugue state, friends continued to materialize and fade, but I wasn't sure who was privy to the news of my alleged potential death. I didn't feel like I was dying anyway because death had a different meaning—living, loving, and losing. Death was no control over my own journey.

I left a lively stint of growth in Portland for Reno after graduating college in May of 2008. The choice was made as I watched friends drop off, pair up, or get accepted into graduate writing programs, which I struggled to get into. In the beginning, there was something romantic about Nevada's honey rock formations, the morsels of sagebrush that swept the east side of the Sierras, and old relic road signs indicating the cannibalistic death valley known as Donner Pass. At twenty-six, a recent college graduate, I had no car and no job thanks to the recession. I sat alone in an apartment far away from downtown in The Biggest Little City while my boyfriend, the Gent, worked. I was a deadbeat but thought as long as I attempted to write, I could consider myself an unemployed artist. I jotted down sentences here and there but mostly languished on the couch, watching a John Waters lecture on Netflix, drinking 40s in the morning while counting cigarette butts as they mounded in an empty wine bottle on the patio. Across the complex, wrens dive-bombed at scattered platters of birdseed. One by one, they came and left, only to make impressions of faint ellipses in the sky and ultimately faded into nothing. It wasn't isolation that bothered me—my disenchantment came from a longer-cast shadow. That relationship.

The Gent was tall, Southern, a year older than me. He was mature, and ate a plowman's breakfast every day with black tea and whole milk, and wrote to his local congressman. He appeared as an upstanding citizen to anyone that met him. He wore satin ties, had a gracious demeanor, and was well-traveled, having spent a semester overseas in Europe and then taught English in Asia. He loved his family. In fact, he had such a strong bond with his mother that he once referred to me as her during a less than appropriate time, if you catch my drift.

That should've been my first warning sign. Instead, I was locked in my own naivety, because on paper, he was a good catch. As I sat sentient in the brand new cream and tan apartment I earned with a good rental history, all I could do was wait for him at home. I sparsely looked for jobs, which only enveloped me more in the long days where the sun never seemed to set. I never wanted to be lonely, I just wanted to be alone.

With each passing day, I watched him from my nest of sheets—unkempt and wearing the same clothes day after day—as he tidily dressed for work between the beige walls in the bedroom of our apartment. Beige is bullshit.

"When the sun hits my body, all I can think about are the prisoners waiting on death row," I said. "I can't imagine what it's like to never feel that warmth."

"Dying doesn't bother me," the Gent said, dismissive, buttoning up his shirt. "It means you start over."

He missed the point, but then again, I had a knack for talking in circles to achieve the perfect metaphor or story arc. It was my way of telling him that I missed my life in Portland, but knowing if I was to go back, it would never be the same. My friends had fled because school was over. I couldn't afford to move back anyway, and what little money I did have was running out fast. Resigning myself to living someone else's life was the only thing saving me from having to move back to Pennsylvania to live with my parents, which I felt would've renounced all the work I had done to get out.

A tour bus just happened to come along one night on its way through Reno, inviting me to hop on and escape after just two months, to drop me with my Aunt and Uncle in Las Vegas.

I was excited about the prospect of living there because the city relished in its own constant parade of delusion. Fake breasts and lavish pool parties adjacent to cheap buffets and penny slots. The rich and the damned. The faux and the favored. I definitely got off on the thought of taking elevator rides alongside random Elvis impersonators.

That was the year the Bureau of Land Management reported that thirty-four feral horses were killed during the mustang roundup. After doing some research, I learned that it was completely unlawful, seeing that President Nixon passed the Wild Free-Roaming Horses and Burros Act in 1971, which enforced the protection of these untamed and majestic equine creatures. While the land had to be managed for farming purposes, for the life of me I couldn't understand why the world wanted to remove or tame something so free. I invented a story about a teenage boy who was sent to a feral horse farm orphanage, where they raised tamed wild horses acquired during the mustang roundups. It was a story that would take shape for several years in my mind, and as much as I tried to write it, it would never fully come to completion, never make it past fifty-three pages.

The only outlet was attending free casino shows of washed-up oldies groups peppered with a few players from the original lineups. My Uncle was a showroom usher. My Aunt went for the penny slots. I went for the free drinks. Though all these performances run together in a sea of blue hair and flattened ornate maroon carpeting, I became obsessed with one Elvis impersonator in particular. He was my age, from Tennessee, was married with children, and his manager was a total stage dad. Though the performer appeared to be happy on the outside, on stage and off, I was wholly convinced that he was a prisoner of his own persona.

DESPITE WORKING THREE jobs and twelve-hour days in Las Vegas, I quickly grew bored. From 4 AM to 1 AM, I played the part of a barista, English tutor, and concert promoter. Reality was taking a toehold, and my dreams, whatever they may have been, began to fade. My Aunt suggested that I go on a date with her neighbor's son. She hadn't mentioned that he was over forty. Or that he had kids.

"It'll be good for you to get out," she said. "It's just a chance to meet someone new."

He was a balding accountant, a turtle with round spectacles. I reminded myself that I was in it for the free drinks and didn't have to drive. I can't remember where we went or what we did, but it took less than an hour for me to uncover his motive.

"She's hot," he said of the waitress, sipping his soda.

I tried not to scowl as I said, "Tell me, what's the difference between me and her?"

Without pausing, he retorted, "Nothing. Both y'all got tits and ass."

I should've slapped him. Instead, as I picked up my handbag to leave, I knew that would be one of many bad dates I would go on for the duration of my stay in Las Vegas.

One date took me to a British pub off the strip. While trying to amuse, or poorly lure, me with pixelated photos of his engorged purple penis with a Prince Albert piercing, a man-child standing at almost seven feet happened to walk in. Long hair, sleeved with tattoos, and a red bandana tied around his neck, he looked like Brian Warner gone grunge. An unlit cigarette hung from his mouth sat down on the other end of the bar and made eye contact.

"I know him," I lied to my date.

He replied, "People come and go all the time. It's Vegas."

I picked up a few dollar bills and headed for the jukebox. If the white v-neck wearing Adonis responded to the right songs, I knew to make a move. Transient visitor or not, I figured I could at least divert from my current situation with a few tunes.

L7's "Shitlist" kicked on. The stranger bobbed his head as his gaze sidled my way. My date, still obsessing over the private porn catalog on his phone, allowed me to look back at the cute guy, catch his gaze, and pantomime hanging myself.

He mouthed inaudibly, "Is that your boyfriend?"

I smiled, bit my bottom lip. (My signature move.) "Noooooooooooo."

He gave me the come-hither nod.

"Later!" I said to my date and pushed the stool out from under me.

When I approached, I stood at his navel. He wasn't a rock star— not even a musician, but a local union plumbing apprentice from

Alaska. Wobbly and drunk at that, which didn't deter my attraction. "You want a ride home?" Alaska slurred. "I've got my motorcycle and an extra helmet outside."

"Thanks, but no thanks."

"Can I have your number at least?" His green eyes gleamed.

I scribbled it down on a bar slip and handed it to him. "You won't remember this tomorrow."

"Oh. I'll remember you."

A COWORKER HAD brought my laptop to the Intensive Care Unit, knowing my obsession with my job. Hazed and dazed, each time I turned to lay on my side, a wrenching pain and nausea made me puke.

"Look away," I pleaded, reaching for the long plastic bag. The vomit was a shade of red. Internal bleeding or a hemorrhage leaking, I didn't know.

When the trauma surgeon came in equipped with a needle and sutures, that was the moment I realized my scalp had split open at the crown.

"Are you gonna shave my head?"

Not my first rodeo. The Chelsea haircut was my thing junior year of high school.

The surgeon combed through my blood-matted hair with his fingers. "I don't think so," he said. "Looks like you'll need only one or two stitches."

I really felt like a wuss now.

As he prepped to sew my scalp back together, I thought of the movie *Hannibal*. The scene where Anthony Hopkins sawed off the top of Ray Liotta's head and was serving him cooked parts of his own brain. I most likely voiced that same comparison to the surgeon as he stitched my head.

My coworker walked back through the curtain. He was also a close friend who worked comics, and we would often commiserate over bad life choices. When he looked down at me, his eyes were clenched and despairing. In fact, for as many times as I'd seen him sad, he had never looked that sad.

"Why did this happen?" I asked him, catching my breath.

He reached for me, fighting tears. Sitting down next to the bed, he began stroking my hand with his thumb.

I quickly fell asleep. I dreamt of a band, that Band. The same one that I always had—that Band so near and dear to my heart that not even the tattoos on my body to commemorate them do my ardor justice.

BEFORE MOVING TO Columbus in 2005, I was sitting in my '99 red Chevy Cavalier, clutching my art portfolio outside the local tattoo shop. I had just been extended the offer of an apprenticeship. There was still an itching in me to get out, to leave home forever. My work was done there, and I knew I could go no further if I didn't grant myself the opportunity to see the world. I had saved up enough money to make one swift move. I sat with my fingers picking at the plastic folder pages, knowing while I was only twenty-three, this could've been my one and only chance to be brave, to finally get out.

My decision to leave home initially was to attend art school in Columbus. But after one semester, I had taken to writing more than my Adderall-stricken schoolmates, obsessed with perfecting their gouache tones and measured matted cuts with rulers and Exacto knives.

Ultimately, I dropped out of art school and decided to move into my own apartment in the Short North Arts District. My very first apartment. I paid for it by working two food service industry jobs within walking distance. It was rickety, but homey, as it came furnished; a humble sectioned-off studio at the bottom of a large yellow Victorian house. About four-hundred square feet, it was lined with outdoor carpeting and sporadic electric supply that shut off when I used the hairdryer. There were indications of mice from teeth marks through rumpled Doritos bags I'd left on the counter. I slept on a twin bed in the kitchen. Decorative wood pillars divided the living area. It had a brown leather couch and a broken fireplace, decorated with a carving of a young boy fishing into the mahogany mantle.

As snow fell, a depression grew. So did the anxiety. I was working over fifty hours a week to keep it at bay. Shift meals and shift drinks kept me from having to go to the store. When the clock hit ten, I'd retire home for an episode of *Dateline* and then continue writing a novel about a city girl overshadowed by her boyfriend, an acclaimed disco dancer destined to be discovered for his talent, until she had captured the imagination of a folk singer who later took advantage of her, which led her to go insane, join a cult, and ultimately die at the hands of mass suicide, alluding to the sacrament of the Peoples Temple in 1978.

Although writing, I only really found solace in booze and record collecting. I already decided the best years were behind me. There was always a bottle that was turning in the leftover stock in one of the bars where I worked. Locked away in my apartment, waking most mornings curled up on the bathroom floor, I still never saw drinking as a problem. I adopted the habit after being prescribed Xanax as a young teen, which was once taken away from me at twenty because I had a tendency to run through the prescription too quickly. My physician called it abuse, I called it necessity. The doctors didn't realize how often I needed it. As a kid, my anxiety left me feeling too small in too large of a town, then state, country, world, and universe. In the night, David Letterman's exuberant quips echoing from the living room would push me to the floor. I'd think about all the unsolved murder mysteries and how the West Memphis Three were wrongfully accused. *What if that happened to me?* I'd reel in so much of these thoughts I'd tremor and shake for hours to the point of exhaustion. So when there was no more Xanax, I had to fill the void when the chronic pangs of anxiety reared. I'd soon find myself consuming alcohol too often.

That Christmas, and throughout the New Year, I sunk further down than I ever had. Drink drank drunk. I realized my disillusionment. Adulting is a cumbersome reality that I would learn takes true artistry to get right. A huge responsibility that I was forced to live in and could most definitely do without.

Come February, snow was caked heavily on the ground, thickened to a crisp that glazed the brown grass, but the Band I loved was coming to town.

Oh, *that* Band... living in their leather jackets without a hint of irony.

One guitarist, a walking homage to a young Bob Dylan and the other, their guitar player, my Crush, *the Crush*, a slicked-back Johnny Cash/Chris Noth hybrid. They came to Columbus that year, when I had grown quite depressed. I was given a CD of their latest album that was a mix of folk, shoegaze, with '60s country construction. I really took to it. And in that, I left the tyranny of the Pennsylvania Dave Matthews junction behind completely. Grace was gone, but to greener pastures.

While working a late-night gig as a hostess at a western-themed bar owned by former riot grrrls, I overheard that same Band was playing a private set at the local radio station. It became my mission to meet the men who wrote the music.

After throwing on my finest layer of mascara and withered, secondhand Paper Denim and Cloth jeans, I drove down to First Avenue across from the local rock radio station and began knocking back vodka at 11 AM on an empty stomach. I was too anxious to be around anyone new, unless out of necessity—social cues didn't come naturally.

After two or three, I sauntered over with my best buzz masked by cinnamon Binaca. The entrance was a glass castle; I felt like a bull in a China shop.

"I'm here for the band," I told the receptionist.

She was a streaky blonde, with stick-it notes fanned out on her hand. "Of course!" she said, asking no more questions. "Have a seat."

I couldn't believe how easy it was, and I silently celebrated how the alcohol vice completely averted my shyness without a blip.

The receptionist brought out the producer. "So nice to meet you," he said.

I smiled. "Yes. Isn't the new album spectacular? The Marty Robbins influence is a major leap from their previous work, which is too reminiscent of The Jesus And Mary Chain."

The sides of his mouth rose with a smile, and without pause, he beckoned me towards the studio door in a warm whisper. "C'mon, they're about to finish."

There, a surge of power that I never knew. Tipsy at nearly noon, about to meet the Crush that I so quietly pined over behind closed doors. *There had to be a catch.* I had to wonder what it was that made these people think I was anything but a fan?

Out Crush came, limbs frail like a metal rake. He looked at me and smiled.

The producer placed his hand on my shoulder as we moved in on Crush and his band, and asked, "How long have you been working in publicity?"

Publicity—an assumption I hadn't considered. Suffice to say, while a simple yet incorrect term, my alcohol-soaked hubris got me to my Crush, and I couldn't help but wonder just how much further being a "publicist" could take me.

NORTH BEACH

IIIIIIIIIIIIIIIIIIIIIIIIIIIIIIIIIIIIIIIIIIIIIIIIIIIIIIIIIIIIIIIIIIIIII

I TOOK SOLACE in San Francisco—which was an accident, really.

After being accepted to earn my doctorate in Social Anthropology from a low-residency program in the Bay Area, it was no surprise that I couldn't come up with the remainder of the loan once I had enrolled. Of course, I learned this after I booked my residency trip. Upon my then-husband's suggestion, I went, just because. This was the beginning of the demise of our marriage, but neither of us knew it yet.

I arrived at the Green Tortoise Hostel the day the bus for Burning Man left. As I was writing in the dining hall that afternoon, after spending hours on Haight plucking pieces from secondhand shops and army-navy stores, the resident cook, a long-faced fellow with long black hair tied back, took me in as a kitchen guest.

"You cut the potatoes for curry, and I'll give you beer."

I agreed. He handed me a knife and I began to chop.

"My girlfriend is coming back, she lives in Ukraine," he said before taking a long pause to stock the kitchen. "She's so beautiful."

The wistfulness in his eyes made me realize what I was missing. I never longed for Ex-Husband the way the cook had for his Ukrainian girlfriend. Whether she had come to see him or had another reason to stay in San Francisco once or twice a year wasn't clear, but his smile told a story of a love that I didn't have. All I had was my job as a publicist.

I just finished up a three-month contract with a local film festival. Though employees spent the vast majority of the time preparing for the intake of film routing and guests alike, it only ran three weeks, but it remains the longest-running of its kind—twelve to fifteen hour days—back and forth to theaters across the city. My job was interviews, junkets, red carpets, and galas for actors, directors, and producers from the US and abroad, some renowned and some new. Though it was a lot of work, that's when I learned to differentiate my job as a publicist from the industry hangers-on and sycophants, that I all-too-often came across when trying to get things done.

There was a cult filmmaker that I referred to as "Salad Sandwich." He insisted I keep everyone—fawning fans and my coworkers—lined up against the wall and at a safe distance beyond the curtain while I watched him hastily consume cup upon cup of IPA. I'm exhausted by people who *believe* they're *that famous*. Industry folks like Salad Sandwich refer to everyone else as "real", which is actually meant as a hit below the belt. But despite their ignorance, real people have way more integrity.

I looked at the cook and asked, "Do you know much about Janis Joplin?"

He shook his head.

I laughed and said, "Guess I'll have to take on this mission."

Specs' Twelve Adler Museum Cafe, tucked away in William Saroyan Place, is off Montgomery Street in North Beach. The perfect bar with lowlights, low ceilings, wooden decorum, and nautical oddities behind glass cases—a place where time seemingly stood still. The most pivotal scene from *Diary of a Teenage Girl* takes place in the back of the establishment, when the young girl in the movie, out drinking with her mother's boyfriend, finds sexual prowess and ultimate control after he gets an erection when she sucks on his finger.

I sat down at the bar and paid cash for a vodka soda. While writing in my journal, a man about my father's age, three stools down, interrupted.

"This is a regular's bar."

Dropping my pen, I rolled my eyes. "Sorry, I'm trying to write."

"What are you writing?" he asked, his voice lifted at the sound of my orneriness.

I was ill at ease seeing that I just wanted to be left alone. "Making notes on Janis Joplin."

He promptly picked up his green windbreaker and moved next to me. "What do you want to know?"

I took a long sip of my drink. When I came up for air, I began chattering about the graphic novel I was working on at the time, about a boy and his feral horses. He told me how he was retired, how he used to book acts at the Great American Music Hall, and alleged that Willie Nelson had eggs and bacon on his rider and that Neil Young's father had a hand in writing *Hardy Boys*. The stranger paid his dues and quickly earned my trust with celebrity inanities.

"The history of Janis is written all over North Beach," he said. "You want a tour?"

My best judgment said no, but the alcohol in my blood and pepper spray in my pocket consented.

WHILE I LAY in the hospital bed alone at night in the ICU, my head swung like a wrecking ball between migraines and nodding off.

"I want my husband," I said to the nurse.

She looked at my chart. No husband to be found.

"You want us to call your parents?"

"No, I want you to call *my husband*."

In this momentary lapse of memory, I failed to recognize that my divorce was finalized a few months before, and I hadn't spoken to my ex-husband since.

There wasn't a falling out, and it's not that our marriage was bad, some people just shouldn't get married. He and I were friends who had met a decade before and we settled once I hit thirty. The music stopped and I grabbed the first chair I could sit on. It was a comfort until I realized comfort was too comfortable. No attraction or fixation. Simply put, conversations waned. In the three house moves we made during our three-year marriage, I hadn't realized until after the divorce that my career was the stopping and starting point to all those life choices.

Between the long weekends, my ex-husband and I spent in Los Angeles or Las Vegas together, he was mostly subdued on the couch smoking weed, playing video games, and eating DiGiorno pizza. I escaped with friends, drinking and going to shows, and when I wasn't working movie premieres or galas, I was at a comic book convention in some other large city somewhere in the continental US. After the first trip to San Francisco, the city became a habit of romantic ideas and self-reflection.

The high contrast of our lives created a palpable instability. While we once enjoyed each other's company during breakfast, as just friends, bitching about our bad dates from the night before, breakfast at the height of our marriage turned into a silent episode of two people reading the weekly paper or staring at our phones in place of conversation.

The silence turned to annoyance, avoidance, and all-around disregard for my vows once I set my sights on someone else, just days before our third wedding anniversary.

Back then, far beyond my understanding, I approached relationships like a game, just like I had with my career in publicity. It was always about the bigger and better and best. And love not only came second to publicity, but to my friendships and personal life as a whole. I was a bad wife and often questioned my ability to love anyone at all.

Shortly after my divorce, I met a writer who I shared a pancakes and greyhounds brunch with, a few cigarettes, and conversation. The Writer's perfectly coiffed silver hair, tattoos, and his indelible knack for turning a phrase—he was a breath of fresh air. I'd forgotten what attraction was until meeting him. His eyes looking at me like I was the first and last person on earth—being attracted to someone for the first time in years, made me feel human, primal. The more I got to know him, and the more things unfolded through text messages, the more I was able to consider fitting this stranger into my life. Weeks later, after the accident, when I was discharged from the hospital, I realized the tables turned. It became apparent that he was not someone who had any interest in me outside of just my appearance or as Chris Cornell put it, an "All night thing."

Karma's a bitch.

CALLIOPE

IIIIIIIIIIIIIIIIIIIIIIIIIIIIIIIIIIIIIIIIIIIIIIIIIIIIII

CALLIOPE. NOT THE Greek God, but a pudgy, redheaded Mario Batali-type who led one of the local bar bands which played at my cousin's wedding reception in the early '90s.

Like every other Catholic wedding in the very same lavish middle-class reception hall, the buffet was filled with mostaccioli, roast beef, and pizzelles. A mix of Polish and Italian-Americans danced about the waxy wooden dance floor while I sat in the back of the hall, upset that my mother made me put on a dress. I was a true tomboy; short hair and always wanting to play in dirt piles. Weddings were not my scene.

Next to me sat my chain-smoking grandmother who comforted herself with a glass of Michelob, while my aunt (who would later work in Vegas for the Liberace estate and then Wayne Newton), turquoise sequins, ate white cake. She mastered the art of dessert devouring without ever once removing a spot of lipstick. Her mouth would arc over the morsel, clamp down on the fork, and she would all so gradually slide it back behind her teeth.

Hiding behind a Pepsi can, eight-year-old me watched the cuter little boys and girls dance about the floor to a cover band. The boys wore suits and the girls in frilly puff-sleeved dresses that came on hangers covered in plastic bags from the local J.C. Penney. My mother would never buy expensive dresses for my sisters and me— not because my parents couldn't afford it, but because they were practical and knew it was a waste of money. This is most likely the reason why I later acquired a taste for expensive clothing that looks like dumpster values.

When the music stopped, the well-dressed children ran towards the stage and sat down at its lip. Curious, I sauntered over and plopped down with them. What looked to be a perfect Catechism class photo, now had a short-haired Polish ragamuffin at the end.

One of the boys looked at me and said, "You can't sit here."

"Why?" I asked.

"Calliope said *only we* can sit here."

My chin plummeted to my chest and I quickly pushed off of the stage, my Payless Mary Janes scraping across the floor in utter disappointment.

GOOD PUBLICITY

||||||||||||||||||||||||||||||||||||||||||||||||||||||||||||||||||||||||||||||

DURING THE HIDDEN Hills wildfire, Kim Kardashian tweeted, "Pray for Calabasas." My first thought was how this is great publicity for the Kardashians, again, and could probably tack on two more seasons of their overdrawn E! series. My second thought was *why* would anyone pray for wealthy homes to be saved when we all know damn well that the insurance company has the fire department headed for the multi-million dollar ones first? Even after watching the episode when it aired, I couldn't allow myself to feel an iota of sympathy for the Kardashians because not only did the fires magically touch just the edge of their property lines, they had the funds to quickly fumigate their houses.

I could go on for miles about the horribly obvious PR tactics of the Kardashians—but I can't say I wasn't susceptible to their media circus. They are brilliant marketers and an epic time suck; *Keeping Up with the Kardashians* served as a distraction from the loss of my child.

My kid was over seven months in gestation when a clot formed in the umbilical cord. First, her kicking slowed, then the kidney pain began. It happened so slowly yet so fast over a three-day period between her death and stillbirth. She was her mother's daughter, going down and taking prisoners.

The night before the emergency room visit, when she died, I was watching the movie *Candyman* while eating a Chipotle burrito, when all of a sudden it felt like I had been kicked in the right side of my lower back. I dismissed the pain and went to sleep, only to wake before the sun the next morning with projectile vomit. My body began to convulse. I turned on the shower and crawled into the fetal position and continued to puke. Any drop of water I drank wouldn't stay down. This amount of illness in the second trimester made no sense, so I gathered myself and shoved off to the ER clinic, and the ER clinic referred me to the nearby Catholic hospital.

During the ultrasound, surrounded by nuns, I was asked, "Do you have a will?"

I looked at the baby's father, Alaska, the long-haired bandana boy who'd offered me a ride on his motorcycle, sitting next to the hospital room window, his head resting in his hand. "Do *you* have a will?" I asked him. I'd never been admitted into a hospital before so I thought it may have been a common question.

Looking back at the nun, her tunic somber under the fluorescent light. "No," I replied.

"We can't treat you here, this is a Catholic hospital. We will have to transfer you."

They shoved me in an ambulance and sent me off; somewhere en route I put it together that Catholics inducing labor was considered abortion. That's when it all faded to black.

If I had been Catholic, would my life have not been spared?

In the neonatal intensive care unit, they tape pictures of flowers on the doors of the rooms of patients of babies who are dying. In the bed, I was hooked up to an IV and a catheter, along with circulation boosters strapped to each leg to avoid clotting. My body puffed up from the excessive protein and blood pressure leap. My hands were the size of Mickey Mouse gloves. I only woke when the nurses came in to take blood for labs, insert more Pitocin, or to check my dilation.

As my temperature climbed, I was too far gone to recognize death—my own or my daughter's. The near-death or dying pins and needles feeling is real, and when you're in pain, as you begin to go, it's a godsend. The delirious state brought me back to the place I knew well and called home in my mind. Each time I closed my eyes, there I was standing at the foot of a limelight stage, the beat of the crowd's feet behind me clamoring at wielding guitars and perfect pitch melodies that resounded in the echo of an unknown music venue. The best high.

Upon waking, my father sat dutifully at my bedside after I delivered a stillborn baby. Feeding me vanilla Blue Bunny ice cream, he said, "Now you can do whatever you want. You can go to graduate school like you wanted."

Pregnancy dismissed.

Deep down, so far deep past the weeks, I had counted on the baby's arrival, I knew wholeheartedly that it wasn't in my life plan. Children were always a big no-no when I considered moving across the country, paying my own way through undergrad, only to be the one with the glittery-glamorous job that would grant me a downtown loft with high ceilings and a closet full of Balenciaga bags; a life where I could go out to dinner every night and see every show my heart desired. On the other hand, I had always dreamt of earning tenure at some private college back in Pittsburgh. A quiet life, living in a big Victorian house in Squirrel Hill or maybe Sewickley, among the grand trees along the river. I'd wear gray sweaters and grow my hair long, preaching the importance of nonlinear narrative to junior and senior writing students.

Alaska didn't know what to say about my pregnancy. I waffled between abortion and putting the baby up for adoption. It stemmed from makeup sex, from a fight that we had when I told him I was looking for another apartment. Or maybe it happened when my parents were visiting Las Vegas that Christmas. At one point, I even went to the abortion clinic, but wasn't far enough along, and the mere thought of going back there made me uncomfortable. There was something growing in me, and whether I chose adoption or keeping and raising the baby, to this day I can't say for sure which way it would've ended had she actually arrived. The demise of the fetus, it went without saying that my life was at a long, hard stop. As my belly grew, I actually took pride in the idea of being a mom. I ate right and exercised, took supplements, and saw doctors regularly. To me, babies were an absolution, ending your own life and its priorities to take on someone else's. There was never a moment during my entire pregnancy that I considered the fact that the baby would simply not come. I never anticipated the complications, let alone severe preeclampsia, which nearly killed me, and ultimately killed my daughter. The baby's death hovers over me.

But that's what happened. I was pregnant and then I wasn't. I tried to reach down inside myself and commiserate with all those before me who had miscarriages and stillborns, yet I found a reeling sadness for children who were unceremoniously taken from them. JonBenét Ramsey, Columbine, Jonestown. I can't compare the loss of my stillborn child to the gravity of those lost in such tragedies, but, no matter how you square it, loss is loss, emptiness is emptiness. For me, pregnancy was here and gone, and left in the wake is nothing but void; my questioning and quiet mourning. What was once there, simply vanished. *No matter how big the heartache, the world doesn't stop for your pain.*

The world may not have stopped, but I did. As if the posttraumatic stress, as if the questions of how and why weren't enough, I was discharged from the hospital with no job, and Alaska didn't sign another year's lease for our apartment. We had less than two weeks to vacate. All I had was a meager severance package from my tutoring and teaching job (the school closed down the following year), and a laundry list of doctor's follow-ups for them to figure out *why this* happened.

I sat indoors and binge-watched *Headliners and Legends* reruns, and bid away on stupid shit on eBay because I didn't care. *How many homemade neon afghans does one person need?* I was numbed by loss, guilted by survival, and dizzied by blood pressure medication.

No sooner than my uterus shrunk to its normal size, I hopped on a plane to meet up with the L.A. Band that sparked my interest in working in music five years prior. You can say that I rocked my way back into sanity and clarity, but what got me was the thing that always got me—life around live music, the life backstage, and hanging around on the tour bus with brilliant and lost minds. Long before I decided to crawl back into saving myself from the east coast stupor and west coast longing, that Band was my touchstone. An inspiration. The beginning of what would ultimately bring me back home again.

LUNCHBOX

||||||||||||||||||||||||||||||||||||||||||||||||||||||||||

MY PHONE WAS passed around by friends while I lay in the ICU. They quietly updated my progress to family and other friends who were out of town. Blondie, who I was heading off to meet before that fateful moment when I was struck by the car, took the lead. She knew well enough to avoid too much conversation with my parents. But one person in particular, one who stayed at my bedside, took it upon themself to call my father.

Murmurs came from behind the curtain of my room.

"I didn't hear the phone ring," I said.

The last thing I needed was for my parents to be a part of an already-bad situation. My relationship with them had been somewhat tumultuous since I was thirteen. It began as no-baggy-clothes, pink hair, or songs that put "motherfucker" in the lyrics. But winding back a bit further, I was always kept from dreaming; from locking myself away in my room and hiding away in my own world. The only place where I felt safe.

"You can't be an island," my father often said.

My ass.

And my mother's epic sigh that was reminiscent of the steam

from a clothes iron or the simmering of a hot tea kettle. Whether it was because the floor wasn't swept well enough, or when I hid my report card because of a bad grade in math, or the time I cut off the bottom of my expensive Hot Topic jeans, that sigh became the gauge of disappointment throughout my life. So I inadvertently emotionally separated from my parents. I was always on edge, anticipating the next unknown landmine where the sigh would underline more wrongdoing.

I inherited that sigh.

For a middle-class family in rural Pennsylvania, the household flipped as my sisters attacked teenage angst in their own way. I was the quiet kid (the "low maintenance" child, as I was often described), who rarely got caught. But my hands couldn't muffle the arguments. I'd put on my headphones and crank up Marilyn Manson's *Mechanical Animals*. My world grew darker and existence smaller. It became apparent that as I turned fourteen, in that little house across from the palace I once thought to be the White House, next door to Laverne DeFazio and Hawkeye Pierce, that it felt like it was every kid for themself.

THE QUESTION AS to whether my parents should fly to Portland to take care of me after the accident was not an option. It had been too long since my father and I last spoke, after an argument regarding Donald Trump's presidency. My sisters took it upon themselves to fly out a week apart to oversee my recovery, seeing I couldn't be discharged without the promise of some kind of home care. I was too exhausted to be angry or disappointed, and it wasn't clear how much it actually mattered in the end—I learned much, much later of their remorse for not being there.

The post-concussive symptoms were unmanageable. Coated in a forced layer of OxyContin, I left the hospital.

Movement was an issue. Any movement. The room always spun.

There was a constant headache. In the mirror, I didn't recognize the person with two black eyes staring back at me. The oblong bruise from the hematoma affixed beneath the skin behind my right ear cascaded down my neck to my collarbone with a faint yellow hue—it was very apparent that I'd been hit by a car.

I tried to sleep. Laid in the dark for days. I only picked my head up long enough when a colleague informed me that celebrity chef Anthony Bourdain had committed suicide, where through selective memory or paramnesia, I managed to draft condolence tweets for past clients. Most were stricken with grief, but it took me several months to process his untimely death, and ultimately break down as I was headed to San Diego Comic-Con.

I had little feeling on the left side of my body, but I worked remotely until the light from my laptop gave me a headache so piercing the whole right side of my face hurt. Like a knife lodged so deep in my head, I could feel the turn of the edge of the blade through my pupil. Getting up and down without feeling like I was plummeting off a cliff was an issue, mainly because I couldn't eat, having lost my sense of smell and taste. Eating was not an option, so I sustained a lax diet of almonds, protein shakes, grapes, and coffee. Being too weak to grind beans for my AeroPress, I would heat water in the microwave and dump a spoonful of Nescafé in the cup.

Worst of all was my hearing. It was like holding a conch shell to your head. Muffled sounds of life outside jarred and confused me. My neighbors decided that the moment spring set in, they would start construction on the second story of their house. I would wake with the sound of sawing wood and beeping trucks backing into their driveway. And there was no taking solace in music. I like it loud, abrasive. I like the teeth-rattling riffs of Melvins and the charge of demanding power chords. I like droning bass. Ecstatic drum fills.

What was music if I couldn't hear it, heed it? The cacophony of the endless whir inside my head confirmed I was no longer myself. Music washed away my emptiness, my sense of homelessness, and gave me hope when I felt lost. For every feeling, there was a song. From "Ana's Song (Open Fire)" by Silverchair to Motörhead's "Killed by Death" the power of lyrics and the muse of chords kept me safe from the pain that the world outside caused. These sounds, combined with blood congealed behind my eardrum, caused a slow ring of watery static that—coupled with my brain injury and inability to follow or comprehend rhythm—prompted me to tune into audiobooks instead.

Patti Smith's *M Train* quickly became a lulling savior. I was late on reading her first book, *Just Kids,* which I picked up waiting for a plane on my way to Florida years before and devoured it whole on my parents' lanai. When *M Train* was released, I was the first in line at Elliott Bay in Seattle. The memoir of coffee drinking and late-night crime shows, with vignettes of love, loss, and moving forward, became the Bible of aging for me. When I turned back to it on audiobook, I heeded Patti as she read in a flat monotone that only a lover of words and understanding of the limelight could appreciate. *M Train* effortlessly moves in between dreams and reality, just as I was, lying in my bed, waiting for all of it to be over.

WHEN MY SISTER arrived in Portland she was appalled at the state of my apartment. It less than four-hundred square feet for what she paid for a three-bedroom house in Florida, and even though I had lived there for months, I owned nothing but piles of clothing, a desk I hadn't used, a beanbag, and a secondhand mattress on the floor.

"Where are your plates?" she asked.

"I never got that far."

"What do you eat?"

"There's Lean Cuisine in the freezer."

The apartment came off as a state of peril to her. The reality was that I had been traveling for months; it's unrealistic to live in a city apartment any other way. The more money, the more you spend— that's the whole point of high price points on metropolitan real estate because no one wants to be holed up in a sardine can. Did anyone ever once see *Sex and the City*'s Carrie Bradshaw stay in her apartment outside of writing or fucking? Hell no. That being said, if I had a larger rent-controlled apartment like Carrie, I would've been less inclined to leave. I considered myself lucky to have had a closet with built-in shelves and a door that led to a wrought iron lean-out patio.

My sister scoffed. "I'm going to the store. This is ridiculous."

I felt no shame in my lack of nesting because my life was way more exciting than hers. A week before I was hit by a car, I was in Chicago at a comic book convention, three weeks before that I was in Seattle at another, and two weeks before that I traveled east to west, touching down in eight different cities following a band on tour. And a month before that I was in Florida. Two weeks before that, my divorce was finalized.

With the head injury though came a long, hard pause. It was difficult to convince myself that the shiners would ever go away, or the spinning, and that I would be able to hear and smell and taste again, but this was all based on what the doctors said. From where I sat, with all that was said, I wondered if I would come out the other side different when this was all over. Would it ever be over?

MY SISTER STAYED in Portland long enough to help me acquire legal counsel. To be honest, I didn't even think to do so. It simply hadn't registered that a driver of a vehicle could hit a pedestrian and the onus would be on the pedestrian to fight for the right to cross the street.

She and I walked the back streets to a nearby coffee shop to meet the lawyer. I was armed with earplugs to avoid the jarring sounds, and sunglasses to avoid full sunlight, my hair down and hood up to avoid attention. The sidewalk shifted and I moved along with it, trying to not fall. Everything was so loud and obtrusive, even on roads that I deemed the quiet ones. Like a baby fresh from the womb, I screamed, wanting to be sucked back into darkness and silence. Light fractals and eye floaters appeared as scorching rays. Inability to balance made me feel perpetually drunk.

Upon settling in the coffee shop, my sister wildly jerked her eyes between her phone, checking work emails, and checking her reflection in the window. She and I look vastly different. Her eyes, the same shade of blue as my own, sat meekly under a fresh set of eyelash extensions. She wore skinny factory-faded blue jeans, a pink floral blouse, and a vegan jacket from Express.

Across the table, I burrowed under a black hooded sweatshirt and my Schott biker jacket—which I was wearing that same day I was hit—which not only saved me but surprisingly came out unscathed, without a hint of road rash.

I loved that jacket so dearly, that after they had moved me out of the ICU and into another room when I was coherent, I asked Blondie to check its welfare. Now it meant more to me than just a fashion statement that projected a badass image in my small frame. The leather jacket was now my sheath, my protector, my hero.

When the lawyer arrived, she was wearing reflective gear and carrying a bike helmet. A good sign. Evidently she understood the rules and the rights of the road to protect those affected by them, by showing no fear as a cyclist. She had a lethal demeanor, scary even.

"How are you feeling?" she asked, scrunching into our alcove in the corner of the coffee shop. "I see you're still having some sensitivity to light."

My sister interjected, "Thank you for meeting us." And looked at me as a reprimanding mom would have for lack of manners.

"Alive," I said to the lawyer, without thinking I'd come off sounding curt. "So there's that."

I felt tears, unaware of where they were coming from, and began to sob.

"It's okay," the lawyer said flatly. "This is normal. You're doing great."

I took a breath and sipped my coffee, which tasted of nothing but I knew I needed it. They both waited for me to speak. I tried to maintain my focus; the unwarranted noise had always been hell, now magnified, to which I'm wholly convinced is undiagnosed Misophonia.

"So tell me what happened," she said.

"I was leaving work to meet a friend who was parked on SE Main at Grand."

"This was during rush hour?"

"Yes. But I cross this street nearly every day to come to and leave from work. Traffic was gridlocked, so I determined it was safe enough to cross."

"This happened outside your office?"

"Yes."

She pulled out a pen and adjusted her notebook on the table. "Go on."

"I was crossing at the crosswalk."

"Marked or unmarked?"

"Unmarked."

"Then what?"

"I don't remember."

LOST ART OF MURDER

||||||||||||||||||||||||||||||||||||||||||||||||||||||||||||||||||||||||||||||||||||||||||||||||||||||||

I USED TO hang out in Ankeny Square in Portland when I first moved there. Across from the old venue, Berbati's Pan, was a slim but wonderful bar. Dark and hipster and romantic. Filled with muted lights, a few slowly spinning fans, and long white curtains that masked the vast windows facing the street. It had the comfort of a '60s album cover. A narrow downstairs and upstairs, I often found myself nestled at the eight-seater bar, waffling between Pabst Blue Ribbon and Sofia Coppola sparkling white wine in a can that came with a retractable bendy straw.

I had agreed to meet a boy there on a second date, whose name and face I cannot remember. While waiting, the bartender, who managed to make a green sweater vest look almost suave, seemed to have taken an interest in me. Before the boy's arrival, we exchanged pleasantries on the Portland music scene, what bands we liked and didn't like, who we knew, and those we wished we didn't know. As it turned out, the bartender, tall with dark hair and green eyes, was also friends with L.A. Band's road manager.

"That guy's a doof," the bartender said, joking.

"Oh yeah, the last time we hung out we went to Tony's on West

Burnside," I said. "I stopped by his apartment before and had never seen so many coked-up mirrors and empty McDonald's bags. Then he showed me a Harmony Korine screenplay he was gifted by Chloë Sevigny—I think that's what he said."

"Sounds about right."

I won't speak openly about the exact nature of my friendship with the Bartender, but we hung out on several occasions, with and without mutual friends from that point on. Late-night board games and cigarettes long after the bar closed. What I do know is that he was intriguing. I'd come to learn that he was a part of the local Portland scene in a much bigger way than he first presented. He was all for the success of *Portlandia*, a TV show sending up the city's hipsters, while I was a naysayer, realizing it'd be the beginning of the death of the city's integrity. Portand was blue collar until the show exploited it's coolness and idiosyncrasies—exposure that resulted in a lot of tourism and tech gentrification, which, in my opinion, made the city suck.

Our friendship faded when I met the Gent and moved away to Reno, stopping in once in a while when making appearances in Portland. But then I went to Las Vegas where I stayed until I lost my baby in 2010, which landed me right back in Portland, back to visit my favorite bartender, for a friendly hello.

Over the music, I leaned in to give Bartender a hug. "I just moved back from Las Vegas!" I shouted.

"What??? You were at Burning Man?!"

The DJ and the Friday night crowd made it difficult for us to hear one another.

"Let's catch up!" he blurted into my ear. "Want to see a movie next week?"

"Sure!"

Next week came and texts were unreturned. I went back to the bar demanding to know, *What in the actual fuck?*

It was after happy hour, so the bar was empty and the energy ominous. The person who entered from the kitchen was a spindly guy with shoulder-length wavy hair; not who I expected.

"Is he not working today?" I asked. "It's Wednesday."

Hollowed, he slung a white bar towel over his shoulder and sighed with trepidation. "He's in the hospital. He was hit by a car."

I didn't know what to make of the situation. Was he driving? On his bicycle? I enlisted our mutual friend to tell me the facts.

Bartender was hit while crossing the street and was in a coma.

Later, I learned that the bartender was in critical condition and had been in a coma for several weeks. He relearned association and some communication through writing on a whiteboard. But there was still internal bleeding, for which they put him under once more to operate. Bartender was transferred to a long-term care facility.

THE LAST TIME I saw Bartender was on his fortieth birthday; a birthday party had been arranged at a local park.

I picked up a friend that late morning before heading to the party.

"While walking my dog, I ran into the tamale lady," my friend said, pulling up the collar on his black shop jacket. "I got two chicken, two pork, and ate them when I watched *Star Trek: The Next Generation.*"

It could've been deflection, but then again, I could never give this particular friend too much credit, and it was otherwise a silent car ride. Oddly, I spent more time convincing myself I was doing the right thing by attending the party than I did feeling happy for him.

Pulling in, summer light cast on the pristinely manicured grass, I saw friends and family gathered together. Some had brought gifts, others ice cream.

We stood idly by looking like the bad friends—the ones without ice cream, without children. Bartender's father wheeled him up the asphalt sidewalk. Slumped over in a wheelchair, his face slack-jawed and blank. I thought, "Who is this?" Once dapper and dynamic, he was wearing a black ball cap, a white t-shirt, and green parachute pants.

"Where's his sweater vest?" I whispered.

Not my finest moment. The initial shock of seeing a shell of a person that I once knew well left me feeling like more of a spectator than a partygoer. I stood back. Each person greeted him, wished him well and "Happy Birthday!" His eyes were wide and confused. A cracked smile of crooked teeth. His face, once defined and chiseled, had been rearranged like an abstract modernist painting. But something still glowed. He appeared happier than I'd ever known him to be.

A young woman skulked up behind us. She was holding a paper bowl of buttermilk ice cream, smiled and said, "He knows something we don't. Perhaps it's the secret to the universe."

A few months later, he was dead.

I think of Bartender often.

HOMAGE

IIIIIIIIIIIIIIIIIIIIIIIIIIIIIIIIIIIIIIIIIIIII

IN AN ATTEMPT to save our marriage, my ex-husband and I briefly relocated back to Pennsylvania to start a new chapter in our life. I worked my job remotely for less than two months before I called it. I started to lose my cool, more or less having to do with his hatred for living in the rural mountain valley and unwillingness to look for work.

When I returned to Pennsylvania from New York Comic Con that October, I felt a huge disenchantment come over me when he met me at the airport baggage claim. Forget that I had just had drinks at Manitoba's or pasta at Caffe Dante with other colleagues with whom I was growing closer to despite the distance; that I had rejoiced in the vast artistic culture of the East Village, and had jeans perfectly tailored in the Meatpacking district. This was my reality—coming back to my childhood city, to a man I no longer loved, in a life I hardly knew. I belonged to my job and the endless travel that came with it. I was living up to the nickname "Gypsy" that my grandfather gave me. I was neither here nor there, just in a constant state of flux.

The next morning, when I handed Ex-Husband his cup of coffee, he remarked on its lack of strength and I blurted, "I want a divorce!"

Dumber things have ended marriages, but at that point, coffee was all that had kept ours intact. He left two days later, and I saw the month out before packing up and flying back to Portland.

That's when I booked several flights across the midwest to follow my favorite band, that San Francisco Band—starting in Columbus, then onto Chicago, Minneapolis, Denver, and Salt Lake City—only then to return to Portland, where my job back at the office and my friends awaited. It was something I had been wanting to do for a very long time but was always too confined by the responsibility of marriage and work and money to do so. They hadn't been on tour in five years. They were playing in three cities where several old friends resided. The other two cities served as writing breaks in between.

The jacket arrived three days before my departure. Opening the box, I had never witnessed anything so perfect. Perfectly worn cowhide with just enough slouch to fit a long sleeve and hooded sweatshirt underneath. The subtle simplicity of the jacket implied calmness and strength. Faded black with silver epaulets and belted at the waist. When I slipped it on, perfection. This was my jacket. The *Highlander* of leather jackets.

"I've been waiting for you my whole life," I whispered, hugging my shoulders.

UP UNTIL BRAIN damage, I'd never been good at relationships.

Being an outcast in my own home as a child continuously reared its head and leaving always seemed to be the best semi-permanent solution. I refused to throw pity parties in my wake but rather crept away into a new city and new life only to find myself reflecting on the how and why later. After leaving Pennsylvania for the third and final time, I knew, even with the gentrification that the Brooklyn defectors were creating, Portland had ultimately become my home by default. I'd become nostalgic for the early 2000s scene with its hippie collective houses that held shows in basements and dangled shoes from the eaves. Portland—where there was no going below 25th on Alberta Street because gentrification had yet to peak. But those days were gone. Even when I eventually moved to Seattle, the city I had deemed home long before I stepped foot in it, didn't fulfill the trajectory of my own growth.

As a teen, I wanted to be in Seattle. The rain, the flannel-wearing musicians, and the quietude of Doug Fir trees. *Hype!*, the 1996 documentary about the Seattle grunge scene, introduced me to the cause and effect of entertainment PR and its potential to be an evil injection of capitalism. Predicated or not, I dreamt of a life that existed long before my arrival, before the lemming crawl of Amazon employees that trickled down Capitol Hill. It was there that I rented an apartment just a few blocks away from the old Pearl Jam house (later transformed into a bar that doted on its fried chicken). I even had a few glorious moments of seeing this or that grunge musician making an appearance at Moe Bar or at the Indian restaurant or at the Sub-Pop 25th Anniversary celebration in Georgetown. I found nuggets in my time living in Seattle. But, in the end, it wasn't enough to keep me there.

On the eve of my thirty-first birthday, I left my office early at Seattle Center for The 5 Point Cafe. There, I ordered a vodka soda with extra lemon, slipped a few dollars in the jukebox, and played Mother Love Bone's "This Is Shangrila" in honor of the late musician Andy Wood. Though none of the other patrons—Space Needle tourists—would recognize it. I saw this as my small homage; a tradition that I carried in my travels, playing the tunes of the lost or forgotten musicians inside the comfort of their favorite bars all across the USA.

I ATTENDED COMMUNITY college after high school and worked at a chicken wing joint. It was a local rite of passage, the go-to for everyone who resided there at one point or another. Three buildings, consisting of an old gas station and a train depot, one menu. Monday nights there was live music at one building, Wednesday motorcycle gatherings in the lot, and Friday karaoke at the restaurant. It was pretty much the only place to go in town.

While my sisters worked the front floor, my tattooed self was sequestered beyond the kitchen in the to-go window. It wasn't the worst job. I mostly worked solo, and on the slower nights, would write in my journal and listen to music. When I worked on Fridays, the managers allowed me to sign up for karaoke and held down the fort as I belted Camper Van Beethoven to an unfamiliar audience for the umpteenth time. I'd stuck around so long that the wing joint began giving me odd jobs: picking up flowers to pot around the buildings, running orders to the other venues or the tiki bar in the back lot, coming up with clever selling points for the marquee or names for new menu items. My work ethic was always strong, even with the most menial task.

One Monday, nearing the end of my shift, I was asked to run a bucket of hot wings and an order of cheese sticks over to the music venue. The door nearly blew open from shock waves forced from the stage. On it, fronting the group, was a skinny, shirtless man, laboriously gasping and blowing into a harmonica. He was young, tattooed, and talented. He had glitter-painted eyelids—obviously not from my town.

The waitress looked at me. "Don't get any ideas," she said. "He's got a boyfriend."

Boyfriend or not, his energy was boundless. I had to know this person. I'd never known a guy with a boyfriend before. Who were they? Who were these people who could come and go and travel and see the world? I wanted to know, perhaps be a part of it somehow. The harmonica player would go on to a series of rises and falls. (Oddly, years later, I'd return home from work to find Alaska watching one of his harmonica tutorials on YouTube.) The last time I saw his embouchure was alongside Rage Against The Machine's Tom Morello at a Rock and Roll Hall of Fame induction show.

A MONTH LATER I was inspired to pack a bag and head south to Nashville. It was my first solo adventure. I was in search of the spirit of Johnny Cash, who was still alive but battling with pneumonia in a hospital outside of Henderson, Tennessee. I stayed at the Opryland hotel.

My grandfather, who had passed away a few years prior, introduced me to the world of Johnny Cash. I began frequenting the local indoor flea market close to the community college I attended, where I could buy Johnny Cash records for $3 a pop. The stories Johnny told in his songs, whether they were written by Kris Kristofferson or Hank Williams or were his own, at times, kept my chronic anxiety at bay. Listening to the lyrics shifted my focus to the likes of "A Boy Named Sue" and "Ira Hayes." And as I entered art school, I caught wind of his new recordings with artists like Soundgarden and Bonnie "Prince" Billy. When I heard Cash's cover of "I See A Darkness" it opened a whole new parallel universe of music for me.

In Nashville, they didn't card me. I made my way to the local Hooters, where I met a bartender who went by the nickname "Speedy" and who, without angle, provided me with a beer. It went without saying that I became a repeat offender during my short stay. On the bus one day, returning to Hooters, a boy with curly hair wearing a Korn hooded sweatshirt caught my attention. He was a French foreign exchange student on vacation with his homestay family. I coerced him into boozing up with me that day and soon enough invited him back to my hotel where we played a friendly game of Gin Rummy and quickly passed out. I woke to a note left beside my bed that read, *"It was nice to have met you. Have a good life."* He had also left his phone number, but I never reached out. I learned that moment that I liked things happening in passing. No close connection, no regrets—just drinks, and cards.

That morning, I packed up my satchel and headed out towards the Opryland mall. At the time, there was a path that led from the hotel past the Grand Ole Opry (where many of the great musical country acts, like Johnny Cash, had played or taken up residency). I ended up in the back parking lot of the famed country landmark, where I saw an open backstage door and made my way toward it. A security guard spotted me and shouted:

"Hey! You! Stop!"

I didn't think anything of it, so I played dumb. "I'm just trying to get to the mall."

The guard said, "Wrong way! You want me to call the cops?! You're trespassing."

I looked down at my feet and kicked the flares of my jeans out from under my shoes. "I'm sorry, I thought this was the mall entrance."

"Bullshit."

"Look," I said, reaching into my bag. I pulled out a paperback copy of Johnny Cash's autobiography. "I'm just a fan. I'm sorry."

"You look like a hoodlum," said the man. "Tattoos? At your age?"

My eyes shied. He looked down at the withered and overread copy of the book I was holding and felt pity. His voice softened. "You know he's just down the street. In the hospital."

"Yeah. I was bummed that I came to Nashville and found out they closed the House of Cash off from the public."

"I won't call the police," he said, pointing forward. "The hospital where Johnny is, it's that way."

Off I went to meet the Man in Black to have the biography autographed. Whether kismet or a calling.

WHOEVER YOU ARE
PART I

A TRAUMATIC BRAIN injury is outwardly unrecognizable. Once the black eyes faded, I appeared normal. But in my head, it was spinning vertigo with each shaky step I attempted to take. Weeks out, I began to feel my life slipping away as I continued in a walking sleep. Holding onto walls to get out of bed, sitting in a plastic chair in my standing shower. Even hand-grinding beans for my morning coffee was more of a chore than I could bear. Determined to go back to work, to feel an iota of the life I thought I'd known, I found myself winded once I got to the last stage of putting on makeup in front of the mirror.

A coworker, who had suffered from her own personal physical setbacks, introduced me to the "spoon theory", a metaphor that used spoons to describe the amount of mental or physical energy a person has available for daily activities and tasks, while my occupational therapist gave me a printout of a triangle that noted stamina to cognition. Still in my right mind, or so I thought, I couldn't fathom fatigue. If I could work with mind over matter, my body would give way and comply with my desire to dredge forward as it always had.

This was not 'mind over matter', this was my brain, exhausted. It seemed a losing battle—but at the same time a concept so foreign, with all my willpower and no-bullshit attitude, that it was a no-contest. I had to have patience if I was ever going to heal.

Getting others to understand this proved to be more difficult. Appearing okay on the outside, damaged on the inside. I started to gain a better understanding of people who suffer from chronic mental illness. Living inside one's head is a terrifying existence, and once the physical external signs subsided, and even when the vertigo began to wane, an overwhelming feeling of displacement made its way back into the sphere.

My employer had complied with my working from home. The inside felt safer than the outside. Alone in my studio, I could only afford to send out for Uber Eats and Grubhub so often. I still needed toiletries, I still wanted to feel sunshine. I mustered up the courage to start going outside and luckily lived across from a grocery store. It took a few weeks to even cross at the intersection alone, but it was just one street. I still had therapy sessions to attend on the south waterfront, which was a $15 Lyft ride one way, and one bus and a streetcar ride from the same location where the car struck me—right next to my office. What was once straightforward was now a stop and start, and the hesitation of head shaking as I crossed in fear. Alert, I felt the breeze, the pavement, heard each and every bird and engine; distracted, it was a 100 percent certainty that something would kill me.

Once I got the patterns down, counting 1-2-3-4 streets I would have to cross to get to a set destination, I was told by my physical therapist, during balance exams at the health center, that exercise would help cease the spinning completely. Looping around the block was not enough and I was running out of DVDs to watch. It was five streets to cross to the library, about a forty-five-minute round trip.

Back streets held a false sense of safety, seeing that electric and eco-friendly cars maintained an eerie silence while in motion, and busier streets I'd refuse to cross unless there were other pedestrians around. Everything was calculated to crossing, times of day, visibility, and my own personal bandwidth. Whether physical or mental, I had become fully aware of the brain's true function—to make everything else function. Mine being damaged was infinitely apparent. But only to me.

One day, while walking down the north side of Stark Street to pick up library reserves, Alice in Chains popped on the playlist. "Nutshell" was our song—me and my high school boyfriend.

I stopped dead in my tracks.

I began to sob.

Uncontrollably.

The first of many painful memories came rushing out.

It was as if he was standing in front of me in his Sonic Youth t-shirt all over again, blurting out *"I don't want to see you anymore."* Melancholy in his deep brown eyes, the heat of his regretful sigh.

I was a teen again, wanting to curl up in my twin bed with Nirvana blasting on the radio, and no one could conceive that it was the end of the world. But I was no longer fifteen. I wasn't in Pennsylvania. I didn't live under my parent's roof. I was thirty-five years old with a Master's degree, a salaried job in the comics industry, with my own apartment.

I could travel. Buy a pair of designer jeans at retail price.

But.

On that sidewalk, at that very moment.

Nothing registered other than what had happened twenty years before.

Not me on the sidewalk. Not a brain injury. Not my age or sense of self.

Where I had been or where I was going was a complete void.

Welcome to the Space-Time DisContinuum—the traumatic brain injury version. My body was a gumband and my brain was on holiday. Still breathing, still functioning on autopilot, just barely, the notes scattered around my apartment reminded me to shut off lights while the calendar tacked to the wall amassed at least four therapy appointments per week along with scratchings of what bills were due on what days.

I tried to fit all my clinical therapy back-to-back to avoid several trips, which seemed to take it out of me more than the actual exercises. My speech therapy consisted of reciting words while listening to birds chirp—not as easy as it sounds. Occupational therapy consisted of sitting in front of a lightboard to prove that my eyes were misaligned; I could not see upwards without moving my head. My physical therapy was balancing on one foot without falling over, followed by massage, where I was told that the muscles in my body would be unconsciously bracing for impact for up to six weeks. I also saw a holistic massage therapist who encouraged me to smoke pot. I whined to a psychologist, too.

At home, I remained nested on my beanbag where I worked comfortably for minutes at a time, taking naps between calls, pitches, scheduling, and social media posts. My whole life was in front of the screen, which my eyes majorly struggled with. Even with sunglasses and screens set to dark mode, reading and retaining information brought on nausea comparable to an empty stomach wine hangover while riding a one-hundred-year-old wooden roller coaster. Fatigue set in quickly. I was numb sans the dull pain in my right ear where my skull was cracked. My occupational therapist encouraged breaks—closing my eyes, breathing, borderline meditation.

If I was to sit and focus on my breathing, I'd just as well pick up a cigarette first. Even then, my brain still mulled it all over. I had to work, I had to live life, I always had to become something more. There was never a moment where I felt I had taken life for granted. Life was now. I never stopped to think, or realize why, or feel sorry or sad except on rainy Sundays. Moving was the only way I could control my anxiety. Now I had to take a break because there was no other choice. My mind was catching up with itself and it was, simply put, on a semi-permanent hiatus. I had to give in and let it do what it wanted—sleep, zone out, and wade its way back to reality.

"One minute I was walking, the next I just started to cry," I said, searching the bearded psychologist's face for news of my fate.

Between a crookedly hung tapestry and the bookshelf, he sat back in his chair, clasped his hands together, and let out a light but long sigh. "When there's trauma, people can start to unconsciously disassociate for protection."

I pulled my legs up under me. "So what does that mean, that it'll happen again? Do I have to go through every single thing in my life that triggered a single tear? I mean, I literally felt fifteen again—explain that, please."

He put his hand up to his chin, framing his face with the L of his index finger and thumb. The white noise in the hallway hummed while the leaves in the crack of the blinds blew gently in the summer wind.

"Do you feel like yourself?" he asked.

"I think I know where I am and what my life is, what I've done to get here, but don't know *who the fuck I am*. I mean, Christ, I don't even recognize my face."

For weeks, I didn't understand my reflection. I'd look back at a "person"—blonde hair, blue eyes, band shirt, skinny jeans, boots. Eyes nose mouth. Hair. Skin. Nothing registered. Not a tear, not a single shred. I'd move, adjust, stare like that famous Groucho Marx *Duck Soup* pajama skit. I may as well have had a body double. Less of a looker than Hayley Mills in the *Parent Trap* without the special effects.

"You haven't lost touch with reality," he said.

Psychedelics. The only time I took LSD was one summer night while camping out at the trestle near the local reservoir. I thought I was way cooler than everyone and took two tabs of acid. Everything in sight morphed and time seemed to float on. After a sleepless night I came home to the news that my grandmother was going to be taken off life support. Still tripping, off to the hospital I went to say goodbye. That shake of reality brought me back down so hard the only thing I remember was the *Today Show* talking about the series finale of *Seinfeld*.

WRONG TOUR

LATE MAY. MIDWEEK. The question as to whether I should or shouldn't have gotten on a plane with a cracked skull was moot. Somewhere in my one-track mind of bouncing about life with this unforeseen accident, the plan was to head out to San Francisco, to see a band. Fly in the day of the show and take the 6 AM flight home so I could still get to work the next morning. I was just a few weeks into recovery.

Faced with the ongoing drain of the hematoma and the burdensome worry of a seizure or stroke, I went in for a follow-up CT scan to check the progress.

"We found another clot," said the doctor in the emergency center.

And back to the hospital I went for a night of observation. No tests were done, but the pain in my head persisted. Tylenol was barely a hero. The nurses gave me a tuna sandwich and some water.

"You need to consider how food intake and hydration are affecting you," they said. "Fuel helps the brain function."

My occupational therapist had already requested I start drinking protein shakes and keeping almonds in my bag to munch on. Eating hadn't always been a priority. My diet was pretty much coffee and Lean Cuisine before the fact, along with the dining out that came as a right of passage with city life. I had to start setting alarms to remind myself to eat since my senses decided to go on sabbatical and nothing could satiate them.

After my grandmother died in 1998, it was like all hell broke loose in the family home. Late-night panic attacks stirred up some kind of control. I was stuck at home or went to school, and hated both equally. So when it came down to it: what I could control was my food intake.

It started as an experiment. Skipping breakfast and onto lunch now and then, soon became narrowing down my diet to four carrot sticks and a handful of saltines. Secretly I prided myself on how little could sustain me, and the psychosis became a major teenage power move. I only ate when I was really, really hungry, and I would *only* eat what I wanted when I wanted it. I successfully carried out this little quiet game of defiant food intake into my twenties. Had a fight? Didn't eat. Had too much else to do. No bit of nothing. By the time I had reached my early thirties and to this day, I notice that I refuse the last bite of anything on my plate, albeit unconsciously, or until whomever I am eating with says something about it.

Eating without taste or smell served up a whole new challenge. Knowing I either had to eat or would otherwise experience extreme fatigue where my brain felt like a pile of pudding, without flavor or a smell to entice appetite, exhibited more loss of control than I had ever felt. Not only couldn't I get the fuck out of dodge—tethered by injury, my therapy, legal reasons, my job, and my lease—I couldn't even hone the desire to eat if I wanted.

After an overnight stay at the hospital, I sought out a second, and a third opinion, to make sure it was safe for me to head to San Francisco. If I couldn't get out for a lifetime, at least getting a day of freedom under my belt would hopefully instill, or even momentarily resurrect, an iota of the independence that had always been my safety net. This was my best chance to gain back the piece of myself knocked out of me the minute I hit the pavement, almost two months before.

The morning didn't greet me as well as I hoped. Like every trip I'd taken before, albeit one now accompanied by a prescription Benadryl to fend off sleeplessness, I threw an extra pair of underwear in my bag and headed to the airport. The ever-present fear of traffic and crossing it to Portland's MAX train couldn't deter me. I wouldn't let it. I began mapping out in my mind how many trains and how many intersections I'd have to navigate between my home and the hostel in North Beach, only to find that the moment I sat down on the BART train in San Francisco, my head felt heavy and my legs numbed.

I texted a friend in Colorado, the only person who knew I was traveling, to let them know I had made it alright. But anxiety flooded me. Suddenly the movement of the train, the phantom knife in my head, brought me to a state of panic. I was convinced that my brain was bleeding. If I could just get off at Market Street and make my way to a bed, I thought, I'd be fine. I was just nervous, this was all new again, but my fear was getting the best of me.

Mind over matter I repeated like a mantra.

Foot traffic. Look out. Go with it.

So I did, but not without extreme caution or awareness. People crisscrossing while on their phones and FaceTime, nonchalant. It angered me, made me want to shout, *"Pay fucking attention people!"* Cars were coming, and not stopping before the crosswalk but an inch or two over it. I had to shut it out.

With each step, the closer and closer I got to Broadway, I began to channel my thoughts of better things up the road. The coffee shop at the fork of Columbus and Kearney Street, dividing Chinatown and North Beach that served the best fucking pour-over on the planet, vintage strip club signs that lined the street like a seedy romance paperback, the tattoo shop where a year before I got silhouette linework on the back of my arm, Cafe Trieste, all the delectable pasta of Little Italy—all the way to the view from the wharf where the Biscoff shop sits. There was still so much still ahead of me, why look back?

TALK IS CHEAP

‖‖

SOMETIMES PUBLICISTS LIE. And some are just plain cold. Making people look good can be difficult, especially when most of those who can afford PR happen to be big businesses. Not much different than an attorney, a publicist's constant cause is to be a neutral who is allotted no opinion or presence. A *good* publicist is not seen or heard anywhere. But I'm a sucker for well-designed packages and have mad respect for excellent copy, but as far as everything you see with how entertainment goes, the news is negotiated. Sometimes in drinks, in swag, in bartering or leverage of shiny things, or simply good luck. It's not always calculated and planned because plans fail. The success and happiness of the journalist and the client are what mattered most to me, always.

Clients can be grateful, and it's most gratifying when they are passionate, and their work means something. But when thank yous are sparse, like with large companies, it's easy to get a high when you see an exclusive you placed in the headlines. Because in the end, the publicist is the last to touch the client's creative work before it's delivered into the world. It's a stressful job that pays in more ways than cash, if you give a shit about namedrops and red carpets, otherwise you do it because you deeply care about a client's success and the passion behind their work. And starting from the absolute bottom, you have to have the cleverness of an A&R rep. You have to extract the nuances and study the sociology of who the work would appeal to. Then you build your contact list, then there's perhaps the fact that journalism has a high turnover due to their successes. If you're going to be a publicist, go for those who care. After working the room long enough, it becomes second nature. The endgame is clear, but when a publicist drinks so much that their kidneys only function halfway, it's time to revaluate the networking strategy. Money isn't everything, I'd rather go to my grave with my karma bank full. Not many publicists can say the same.

So where does that leave most publicists? Some in a furious cell of quietude with only stories to tell those who give a damn about the celebrity lifestyle. A celebrity is just like everyone else except they choose to be a public figure, and, in the end, can lose their freedom to the limelight.

OLD PORTLAND

||||||||||||||||||||||||||||||||||||||||||||||||||||||||||||||||||||||||||||||

MORE OFTEN THAN not, when things went wrong, I ran. It was a conscious and planned decision to move from Columbus to Portland, as well as every move I made between 2008 and 2010. These were bleak years. Lost years. While I managed my creature comforts by writing at the nearby coffee shops or taking up temporary craft ideas, the lostness I felt in my initial move to Columbus and then in Nevada, both Reno and Las Vegas, was palpable. The breadth of my adult self was found in Portland, and I knew I had to go back, but Portland was quickly changing.

Still, with limited jobs and increasing rent, there was a brief stint of about six months in Anchorage with Alaska's family. Talk about a personal hell. When my MFA acceptance letter came, I jotted down a plan to reclaim personal sanity:

1   Rent an apartment in Portland's Alphabet District
2   Don't work, only write
3   Chant or practice Buddhism
4   Light candles at The Grotto, weekly

Got two out of four, not bad. But the vintage studio in the Alphabet District was much too small for Alaska and me, even smaller with the emotion that filled it. Day in and out, Alaska sulked over the baby while I scraped by to make ends meet.

We briefly got engaged—a total void-filler—and as I started making plans for the wedding, he simply sat me down at a coffee shop and said, "I don't actually want to get married, ever."

That was that.

We split and it was just me and Portland again.

I wondered what the addictive appeal of the once-quiet northwest city was. Had it been the history, or my growth?

Portland was a small and artistic community, working-class— where those in their twenties and thirties went to work two jobs as baristas or bartenders, or maybe lucky ones like myself who took college courses and worked meager semester jobs tutoring and filing mail on campus for drinking dough. With $5 punk shows omnipresent and a record store that is open till midnight, it appeared as though Portland had a pulse like San Francisco in the '60s or New York in the '70s. It looked like it may have been the dawn of the return for Burt Reynolds mustaches and women in mom jeans paired with white tennis shoes. But I digress. In 2006, everyone appeared individual, creative, and the city was illuminated with talent.

There was a group of twenty-year-olds who hung out on a low-pitched roof of a 1930s Craftsman on NE Pacific Ave. The place exuded mystery. Strange ceramic figurines stood sentient in the windowsills. And in the spring, they'd arranged lawn chairs on the sidewalk, drank Pabst tallboys, and had their shoes dangling on the eaves. It seemed almost natural to waltz into any one of these communal art houses and open their fridge to grab a drink. There were always shows in basements, $1 peanut butter sandwiches, or $1 mohawks on the Alberta Art walk. Everyone got along, it was very Haight-Ashbury, or what I dreamed that Haight-Ashbury was once like.

Once I stepped foot on Clinton Street, in Dots Cafe, on Concordia University's campus near Alberta and the Hawthorne District, I felt right at home. Then and there I decided that I never wanted to leave Portland. It's where my life would be and where I would stay forever. Then again, I never thought of inflation, increased population, or the prospect of tech as an industry wave arching its way up from California. The roses bloomed in February and I-5 signs easily summoned north to Seattle. I was close enough to visit, but far enough to make a life for myself, away from the grunge dream. I could simply spend a night or a weekend in that piece of my youth without deterring the unknown and exciting future. It all seemed perfect, and it was.

Days were spent at school and the nights summoned me to rock shows, outings, and after-parties of the local musicians I came to know—some basking in fame or current; others on the verge of making it big in the indie or underground music industry. I was shepherded into this by bands I met back east—recognized for my ability to promote coupled with the art of working a room. My rules always were to stand to the right, never stay too long, and never say goodbye. Sometimes at Tube in Chinatown, sometimes at the Odditorium or Slabtown, I never made it known where I was going or where I'd be later. I liked being a floating enigma and relished the company of those around me; oftentimes not even engaging. It was a close-up study on cool I'd later use for leverage. *Who's the manager? Who's the guitarist's brother working at the Pepsi distributor? What band will work with that local producer, who works at that music shop, or who might get first billing at Crystal Ballroom? Who's playing Berbati's with the band that is honing in on the next big sound?* Finding where they all were was one thing, either by flier or MySpace, but figuring out the pecking order was another. It's always easier to be triaged from the bottom instead of clamoring all over those at the top. Another PR ugly truth, I know, but a really good publicist always takes notes while behind the proverbial curtain. Don't speak unless spoken to, don't do a thing that draws attention. Be kind, always. If you act like you're supposed to be there, you are supposed to be there. Stick with black skinny jeans, an old black t-shirt, and the slightest schmear of Ruby Woo lipstick.

Parties didn't always come without follies. The pink fuzzy bathroom at the Odditorium, dabblings at Dunes, C-list Hollywood appearances in the Waffle House basement, special access to the balcony at Hawthorne Theater, secret rock star DJ sets at Jarras— all now ancient history. I was never seen in the scene like Sub-Pop publicist Nils Bernstein or Michael Musto of *The Village Voice*, but once had a very memorable run-in with a beloved icon and a fabulous former Club Kid (the reason for my PR success, I think, thanks to their book that became my cliff notes on the glitterati).

It was a Wednesday night at a local dance club, which also happened to be the venue for a YA book signing (yes, you heard me correctly) for said Club Kid. Dressed to impress, donned in my best attempt at Edie Sedgwick in addition to French pinned hair and plastic platform heels, I presented my book for an autograph, which he inscribed, "To the prettiest girl at the gay bar—yay-yay, chop-chop!" He invited me to join his table for a drink and introduced me to his straight friend, an industrial gothic DJ. Three beers and a share of lipgloss later, the club remained empty and quiet. The limo was summoned for us to head to The Jupiter Hotel, where notoriously nothing good ever happens.

Climbing in the door, my heel caught, peeling back a large portion of the paint from the plastic.

"Did you wear those heels because you have daddy issues?" the Club Kid joked, hastily readjusting the baubles that decorated his neck. He crooked his neck to peer out the window. "Portland is ugly and it sucks."

I made a face. Strike one.

I fixed my attention to the radio playing "Come As You Are".

He continued: "Driver, can you turn down the radio? I *hate* Nirvana."

This is why I'll never meet another hero of mine again. No one can ever live up to the image that someone else built in their own mind.

WHAT THEY ASK when it comes to filing a lawsuit. From my personal account and avid questioning of "Did you run across the street?" NO. From wanting my tax statements dating back five years and social security earnings, where I realized in 2013 I made a whopping nineteen grand. I can't tell you how many times I've worked for free— or for show admittance or beer—PR isn't something you can teach, it's learned and, if you are lucky, innate. So, what was I doing in 2013? Ask someone with a brain injury—I barely remember an hour ago unless it's written down or a reminder is set on my phone. From what I can conjure up, I'd spent most of the year unemployed and job-hunting and then landed a position recruiting long-haul truck drivers. At least I *think* that was 2013, according to my 1040. The question was whether I worked towards the goal of my career my whole life or not. Give or take five universities until the right one stuck. While my interests are in entertainment publicity, my degree, I suppose, is a very fine fit.

Around the time that I was wrapping up my undergraduate degree, my interest in the limelight began to fade. Many of the people who I had come to know in the music industry began to struggle. In their off time from touring, they were driving cabs and working in call centers. With no college degrees or skills applicable to the real world, those jobs were a mainstay. It was then that I really started considering my future, regularly talking to a professor who encouraged my passion for writing.

"Maybe you should consider teaching,'" she said, beneath a Radiohead poster, patiently waiting as her Starbucks latte reheated in the microwave. "You'll need a Master's degree of course." For the short term, after being rejected from too many programs, right before moving to Reno, I decided to take a short postgraduate certification course in Teaching English as a Second Language. At the time it seemed like a small step in the right direction; getting teaching experience that could only enhance continuing education applications and job prospects. I felt that I was talented enough to teach the craft, but like I always do, I'd take the longest route possible to facilitate the unfurling dream. *Now* was always the most important since I never knew which direction tomorrow would take me.

It wasn't too long after I finished the two-month course that I nabbed a tutoring-turned-teaching job in Las Vegas. The downside being I had to leave Portland. At twenty-six, I had to be a mature adult, or at least cloak myself in the image of one. Student loans and credit card debt were piling up and the uncertainty of my future was all too palpable. What was once a success story of pulling myself off of the floor of my Columbus apartment and getting myself into school, seemed almost like a mistake. But I remained positive, it was only the beginning of the rest of my life.

FOR WHAT IT'S WORTH

IIIIIIIIIIIIIIIIIIIIIIIIIIIIIIIIIIIIIIIIIIIIIIIIIIIIIIIIIIIIIIIIIIIIIIIIIIIIIIIIIIIIIIIIIIIIIIIIIIIIIIIIIIII

FOUR MONTHS INTO working from home after the injury, bouncing back and forth between the rehabilitation center and sparodic visits to the office, recovery continued to saunter along at a snail's pace, I found myself stuck between the realms of a brain injury and work. Time was limited, as all my waking hours were split between what *had* to be done. I was tired of focusing on eye exercises, how long I could sit in front of a computer screen, the delineation of audio and visual focus, the overwhelming burden of forcing myself back into society.

Change came with comic books. Most of my colleagues were social drinkers. I, at the time, was sober and lacking the desire to devote even more time to talking about comics or a brain injury. The Portland comics industry is a small pool of folks, just like any other facet of entertainment. It's potentially controversial and paralyzing, with a lot of publishers limited in staff, shuffling from comic book convention to comic book convention, whilst at the same time balancing what's current and what's in the pipeline for up to nine months ahead. It's a complete demand of time and effort. As a publicist, being last in line and in charge of the marketing of comic books, I can say now that working in-house with a publisher consumed me.

I aways had a penchant for nerds and nerdom, and in 2016 my networking chops and affinity for sequential art found its niche. When promoting bands and filmmakers that were more divas than doers, my thoughts turned to the unsung creatives of the comics industry. Exactly how many writers and artists were known for their craft in such a métier? Stan Lee? Frank Miller? Alan Moore? Like the garage bands I used to see back at American Legions and random basements, I wondered whether there are talented folks hunkered over drafting tables and Word documents in this endless realm of pages and panels? Could it be possible to facilitate an all-new roster of celebrated creatives in this underground comics subculture? If so, how fucking punk rock would that be?

I fully established my credibility as a publicist through projects I'd taken on over the years, from silver screen to print and vice versa, starting with licensed titles like *Aliens* to Nintendo and comics announcements for *MST3k* (who I worked with prior to their live theater appearances). There was publicity for the series in conjunction with thrash metal band Slayer, while I marveled at the opportunity of working with Anthony Bourdain and Margaret Atwood, and along the way, jump-started a number of new careers for up-and-coming comic book writers. It was the originals and collaborations in the publisher's catalog that most interested me, which is why I went from one publisher to the next, grappling to take part in something fresh. I found that place in 2017 and was right outside their HQ when the accident took place.

While in recovery, I remained dedicated to keeping the train on the tracks with my career; maintaining professionalism to the point that no company or comics creator would be affected by my own personal setbacks. I didn't realize what cost this would have on my recovery. I was responsible, not only for myself, but also for people's livelihood. All things considered, it was difficult for me to separate emotionally from all the passion that comics writers and artists and colorists put into their work, and knowing I was the brunt of their support, I had to keep going.

INSURANCE DENIED THE initial claim, after finding me 51% at fault for the collision. This didn't come as a surprise to my lawyer considering there was no camera footage, and the Portland Police Department's report was scant. The Incident. This was not a slice-of-life tale; had I died on the scene, it would be involuntary manslaughter. Instead, in life, it was an "incident" and nothing more.

I was in the lobby of my local tattoo shop when I got the news. In the police report it said I was "coherent" and "uncooperative" which couldn't have been further from the truth considering the circumstances. It was a shock. The only thing I remember of the police officer himself was when he handed me a business card while I was lay inside the ambulance. How could someone be cooperative let alone coherent after just being hit by a car? I know myself I make light of every weird situation that's bestowed upon me. Maybe it was the quip of "Portland, duh!" when they asked me where I was while still flat on a busy street at rush hour, not fully aware yet somehow able to marvel at the irony.

Worse off, it came to my lawyer's attention that there was zero follow-up with the eyewitnesses or those who made 911 calls. She pragmatically and justly made her inquiries to the witnesses, all but one who was a coworker of mine. And when she tried to contact the police officer, the results came up nil. It was fishy. I took the stance of being hit by a republican who had taken one look at me with my septum ring, tattoos, and a leather jacket and deemed me worthless.

One of my coworkers, sat next to my unconscious body, holding a paper towel to my bloody head, thanked the person who hit me for not running off. My coworker confided: "Not like they could've, you were blocking their car." In hindsight, I'm not sure they would have stayed given the opportunity to run. I also caught wind that they had mentioned they had no idea from which direction I had come, and later insinuated they may have been on a cellphone. Regardless, it was all hearsay; such information was lacking on the police report.

What I did get from the paperwork was the person's name, which once home, I immediately Googled to discover someone I could perhaps have *liked* under different circumstances. It's amazing what we can learn—thanks, internet! *Whoever you are.* I knew I was just as wrong to pass judgment on them as they and the Portland police officer had on me. I may have looked like a plebeian to someone who didn't understand my jacket retailed at $750. Nor was it obvious to look at me that I put myself through college or worked my whole damn life to hone a career that helped other people to realize their dreams. Or that I was simply on my way to spend an ordinary evening out with friends to eat pizza and see Judas Priest. (Judas Priest are no strangers to misjudgement. Hard to believe they were taken to trial in 1985 over supposed subliminal messages in their music after two teens committed suicide, and were forced to argue a case for artistic integrity. More unfair judgments based on appearance, I feel.)

Something else that I discovered: The car that hit me was a rental because the driver's own vehicle was in the body shop, having been involved in a wreck two weeks earlier.

SOMEWHERE DOWN
THE BARREL

||||||||||||||||||||||||||||||||||||||||||||||||||||||||||||||||||||||||||||||||||||||||||||

DISSOCIATION IS SCARY. The parietal lobe is the cavern that connects to the hippocampus, which is in the temporal lobe. With mine damaged, I lost the creature comforts of reminiscent smells, tastes, and most of all, sound, for some time. Causing a focus that's so perilously consuming of my time. Songs have always granted the grand ability to put me into places; when I was able to recognize the song structures, chords, and lyrics again, feelings so real came flooding back as if I was there, back in time, pushing a pocket of a forgotten life and self. This was why I broke down on that sidewalk on Stark Street before seeking therapy.

It went quiet after that. I can't explain the lost time travel. It just unfolds and is presented as if it's here and now. One morning, I was watching the movie *Lady Bird* and Dave Matthews Band came on the soundtrack. It opened up a memory from when I was nineteen—working at the chicken wing joint, dating a thirty-year-old who followed Dave Matthews each and every summer as if he was reaching to touch the hem of Christ's garment. It was a time I hated, long before

I knew myself, before I knew I could be someone or something more than the cowtown podunk sissy I felt like. That summer, I spent a camping weekend for two shows with him and his friends—other people we worked with. I was the youngest of the group. I crouched beside the wheel of his Jeep and sipped on amaretto sours during the tailgate party in the parking lot before the show, snacking on a trail mix he called "gorp." The weather was musty and warm, just like all Pennsylvania summers before and after, feeling the humidity of the pending rain. Raccoon Creek State Park, where we camped, is nestled in a stretch of the Allegheny mountains. I was the youngest and shy. I only spoke when someone spoke to me. Hearing "Crash Into Me" on the *Lady Bird* soundtrack brought me back to that moment, that place, those feelings, as if they were a current space, even though there's no sense of the people or place anywhere in sight. My heart broke for the loss of that moment, the naivety of my younger self. This was not the mind's eye—the mental faculty of conceiving imaginary or recollected scenes—it was an unwarranted feeling of teleportation through time.

CONSIDER THE PRESENT as a 33⅓ or 45 RPM record. If our thoughts stay at either speed, we would be living in the present. The problem is that our brains tend to drop down to 16 RPM because we think about the past, or speed up to 78 RPM because we think of the future. Whereas time, outside of our own perception, never slows or speeds up, it just ticks away. Thoughts are nonlinear because they tend to skip over one another; time is still a fundamentally linear concept. Time moves forward while our personal experiences, individual sensory reactions, backgrounds, genes, dyadic and group relationships, all ricochet against each other to determine who we are in the moment. Our minds work in a stream of consciousness, so thoughts often pop up in random sequences. The senses tend to intercept and change brain patterns, causing random thoughts or misplaced understanding.

It was obvious I was living out my Master's thesis on nonlinear narrative, which started with a setlist of songs that could potentially map my mind through stories, through phases in my life. If I put them in alphabetical order and used page breaks or the right numeric system, I was convinced that some sort of linearity from the abstract construction would come about. When I turned the draft in to my professor, I was told I had to delve deeper. I had used published examples of how this type of narrative *could possibly* be cohesive and understood by the reader: Alistair McCartney's A–Z methodology in *The End of the World Book: A Novel*, Elizabeth Wurtzel's internal versus reflective narrative using italics in *Prozac Nation*, and the ever so infuriating pagination of David Shields' *Reality Hunger: A Manifesto*. But my own content, as a stand-alone, still lacked in the narrative I hoped to convey. Had I a brain injury at that time or foreseen that I would in the future, I would have avoided trying to make sense of the above, knowing in a sense that I was penning my own fate.

In *The Art of Memory*, Frances A. Yates outlines both storytelling and historical records before the printing age and even before the development of writing. Yates focuses much of her discussion on the role of the so-called "locus," an artificial memory that is established by recollecting images, which orators of the past used in their reportage to simulate natural memory.

A Google search informs me that disassociation is a lack of continuity between thoughts, memories, surroundings, actions, and identity—how this applies to both nonlinear narrative and a traumatic brain injury is uncanny. Like stalled text messages between two people over the course of a year, no thought ever has clear linearity; disassociation, without will, in time or space, is impossible to navigate when and where an instance will surface. Truncated. White spaces. What one considers mental clarity, could be another person's ignorance when it comes to having space in the brain.

ONCE I WAS able to listen to more than the euphonious audiobooks without the muffled swish of blood that congealed my ear, I forced myself to open up audio files of music to transport me back, hoping to make sense of, and build a cohesive timeline that I hoped would ground me back into the current reality.

I went back and listened to albums released in 2017 and 2018 to see where it'd take me. Nothing. Even though I had followed one of the bands across the country after my divorce, saw friends, and made new memories, I felt nothing. I tried listening to the album and looking at photos stored on my phone to spark any invocation of an emotion—longing, happiness, sadness—but still, nothing. I went further back, auditing my catalog. It was a practice to blueprint the map, but even then I realized I had to let my mind run its course. It was fighting me as much as I was fighting it, pushing and plugging.

Had my job completely defined me to the point where my only sense of recognition stopped at being a publicist? In PR, some lack emotion to support. It was an accidental lifelong career choice and took great effort, but if I was not *me*, how was my brain only tuning into that aspect? I'd flown the co-op. Just as my brain had shut off all ability to taste and smell to conserve energy for more necessary tasks, it simply decided to shut off my memory. Or the feelings reminiscent of memory. Reaching for moments, such as where I was when I lost my virginity, to what it felt like to have my very first apartment or get into art school or meeting celebrated actors I'd been spearheading PR for, something that meant anything at all, emotions stood gray.

In big business, true neutral is what separates the publicists from the flunkies. Maybe I wasn't feeling anything at all for myself just as I had dampened the excitement to be neutral to get the job done. This is where I had to consider my feelings. But I only *knew* it was broken and I *could* feel sad, but the tears and the understanding of why just weren't there. I felt...nothing. I didn't have to question if this was a concurrent result of the injury, I just *knew*.

It was time to spark a flame. If my mind was not allowing me to move backward, I had no other choice than to go forward. So, one of many three-month-long sober days into recovery, I did as I had always done when looking for inspiration—headed straight to the record store. And the album, Funkadelic: *America Eats Its Young.* The song: "Biological Speculation." While I wasn't hungry or no longer felt ostracized by the society that my teenage self felt so spurned by, the lyrics spoke to me. Songs belong to the listener. If I was going to let myself sit idly by while the person who hit me with their car and took everything I knew away, taking no responsibility, it was still my will to fight and move on. My body fought, it wanted to keep going even though the injury itself could've ultimately killed me.

The question of why I wasn't dead or why I didn't sustain a permanent handicap or mental retardation wasn't a question of will, it was luck or perhaps, biology. I knew, listening to those lyrics, that something far down inside me—an edifice I couldn't even touch—kept me coherent to some degree. Justice would find its way somehow. To paraphrase Funkadelic, I was "vibrating" with an "animal instinct." I wasn't giving up.

PRESENT TENSE

||||||||||||||||||||||||||||||||||||||||||||||||||||||||||||||||||||||||

IN LOSING MY mind, I was surprised at how far I was stuck in it. As each cavern opened and unfolded a memory, I still struggled to understand the here and now. The good news is that my gears were turning, searching, trying to make sense of where I'd been and who I was to put a stake in who I'd become—why it all happened—a mild cognitive setback. My brain compartmentalized everything to heal itself, so any hint of memory or a triggering emotion was more than I could bear.

Author and spiritual leader Ram Dass said, "You can't be in your thoughts anymore because your thoughts are still time and space and you can't get out of time through them." I had to take a mental escape and challenge myself despite the setbacks. In between working and a brain injury, where was I? Imprisoned. I could've joined a book club or taken up knitting to occupy the few moments I had to myself, but reading made me nauseous and knitting was for moms-to-be or those quitting smoking. All my friends worked in comics, so it was difficult to escape the ubiquitous work conversations.

My tattooist is an artist, not a therapist, tattoos are expensive, and the last time I'd seen him he had given me three runes for healing, to end strife, and good health—relative to getting through the accident. It was time to make new friends and what better way than the temporary distraction of dating apps.

Ugh. Dating.

So, I haven't been as crystal clear as I could've been when it comes to my past relationships. There's no point in taking a crowbar to the proverbial coffin when perhaps you have one too many skeletons branded with your name.

Many of the relationships I started in my twenties could've been good ones if it wasn't for Crush. Crush—who, after that one fateful "love at first sight" incident at the radio station back in Columbus in 2006—turned into a chain-smoking, coffee chugging one-on-one after his show that night.

Which provoked me to share a copy of my then-book.

Which inspired three songs on his subsequent record.

Which transpired into a more frequent emails.

Which became "I'm in your your city, let's hang out."

This is the abridged version, but it carried on for twelve years.

Those promising young ones I dated were left in the wake.

I had never wanted to be anyone's girlfriend because, since I had first laid eyes on Crush, that was it. Even though I saw him only every now and again, twice a year at most. I tried to hold down the normalcy of going to college and dating common people (audacious, yes, but for a lack of a better term), no one was going to compare to the image I'd built up in my head of Crush. So each time, right before he came around, a breakup commenced.

WHAT WAS IT about him? Everything. An alluring Aquarius who spoke softly and laughed shyly at his own insecurities. For as much celebrity as Crush had, he remained humble and human. He had grace.

A charming wit and a beautiful mind that exploded with enviable creativity. He fed something in me that was of the summer wind. I knew he would always leave, so I could breathe; no expectations.

What never occurred to me was Crush's life. Rock star, family man, or whatever. Because of my lack of understanding, his gestures became haphazard at best.

One night, under the security light of a venue parking lot in Salt Lake City, he said, sweeping a sweaty brown lock from his brow, "You're finally the person I'd always hoped you'd become."

His proud look, almost predatory, sent me reeling. Reeling through all the ages and things I had passed by and potential lives I could've been living and chose not to. It came down to that very moment.

He moved in to grab my hand—I retracted.

"So you waited until I was ripe? What—the fuck."

I felt like *Georgy Girl*. The scene where James Mason so proudly proclaims that he once viewed Georgy as a daughter, but had grown to be very thankful that she wasn't and then propositioned her to be his mistress. That film still has me reeling just as much as that final moment with Crush. I don't belong to anyone and don't want to.

So much for indulging in romance. At least I got a few songs out of it.

I MADE A dating profile and created a few rules: no talking about the brain injury or work, and most of all, don't get too close to anyone. It seemed to make sense; I was in no condition to involve myself because I was nowhere near my right or normal mind. It was simply an experiment to challenge myself in new situations, to meet new people, and to be inspired to get out of my head.

At that point, I was sober for three months. I heard an array of cautionary tales from head trauma doctors and therapists alike, but it was me who stuck to the cold, hard rule of sobriety because I didn't want to mush up my already-mashed brain. I feared that I'd end up like those people who suffer from addiction and remain the same age as the year they acquired that addiction. Plus, drinking and comfort always seemed to go hand in hand in new situations, or the art of working the room as a publicist, or the all-around post-work or bad relationship bitch sessions. Maybe trying something different wouldn't be so bad. Like switching to smoking pot (CBD for pain and THC for lucid calmness), kombucha wasn't cutting it.

The app uncovered a world of tattooed writers and musicians. Body art opened the floodgates for easy conversation. A simple commonality creating an exchange of topics, everything from rememberence pieces like crosses with death dates to other pop culture adoration—nearly a scapegoat. You learn a lot about a person from their tattoos, and those with tattoos are easier to identify with when you have many as I do, as opposed to someone without. They have reasons, are not ashamed to wear their jokes, passions, or pain on their (literal) sleeve. Ironically for me, tattoos were mementos affixed to my skin so I could never forget who I was. From the first Kill Rock Stars logo from when I was eighteen, all the way to muses and homages to the music that kept me inclined to live for so many years. They all meant *something*. Even as I drifted away from my art school fascinations with folk artists Elliott Smith and Nick Drake, their mugs still stare up at me from each shoulder. Tour tattoos, to the tiger lillies that serve as filler on my forearm to remind me of the fields beyond my childhood home, to the mighty words LIVE THROUGH THIS bannered across my chest for the HOLE album I loved and the kid I lost. My past is all accounted for in ink. If you can't wear the battle scars on your body, you may as well hide in the forge.

On my first date after the accident, the dude had *Invader Zim* on his shoulder, allegedly graduated from Portland State with a degree in psychology, and after being laid off from a job at the hospital, took a job as a cook at a strip club. The second date had a smattered sleeve about which he said nothing, but instead the financial security that came from touring with his commercially successful band every summer. He talked about his new car, how much money he had in the bank, that his parents didn't share his liberal mindset—which made it all too obvious where this was going. As he rambled on about the future he intended, wanting a wife and kids, I stopped the waitress and asked for the fanciest drink in a martini glass. One, two, three sips, sitting in the cushy vinyl booth with the summer light creeping into the dark bar, I sensed homeostasis: nowhere near interested in the guy or what he had to say, but in the liquid flow of comfort that the alcohol gave me. The background noise began to fade as did his rambling. When the check came, he asked to split it, I obliged and we parted ways, never to see each other again.

Dates came and went, from pinball to amateur wrestling. No talk of bad brains or good comics, no goodnight kisses or hand-holding, it stayed platonic throughout. I'd talk about where I went to school and writing, what bands played the best sets in certain eras of their careers, and my dates shared their knowledge of guitar gear and some wrote short stories of their own. It was a nice escape.

But the moment I felt their attachment, of wanting more, I would end it. They weren't just looking for a temporary friend or even a distraction from life like I was, they were looking for love, longevity, and someone to call home. Once I came to this realization, I felt terrible about my motives. My calendar included other dates to come, but thankfully a few had already made excuses and bailed out. One said his wallet was stolen so he couldn't meet, another reneged because he said he didn't think we had made concrete plans. I'd pretty much exhausted this grand experiment because I learned that going out again, going to happy hour to commiserate with my friends, *was* an option.

One Sunday afternoon, I met up with a friend for coffee. As he grabbed the cups and we headed for the back patio, my phone buzzed. It was a text message with a brief and friendly hello, accompanied by a mischievous monkey emoji. Someone new, someone I knew nothing about, but someone *I knew*. This person, what I didn't know but would find out very soon, was my Soulmate.

KOMBUCHA BAR, SUMMER 2018. I had borrowed some money from my mom to help with paying for the Lyft fare to and from doctor's offices, which ended up shuffling into other dollars, so I most likely spent some of it on a haircut.

Soulmate texted to tell me he was going to be late. I stopped to refill my CBD cartridge. He texted again and said he was parking—by then I was three sips into my rosehip kombucha.

Sleeved in tattoos, nose pierced, big, long beard, he was hard to miss, though not as tall as I'd imagined. I gave a gentle wave as he filled his cup. He sat down next to me at the small wooden table.

"Sorry I'm late," he said.

"I appreciated the play-by-play," I said, smiling.

It was like the sun yawning among the hills after a long night's sleep. Something was different. Then I realized it. *I could smell him.* I don't know if it was the strong scent of patchouli or if it was pheromone detection, but it was immediate—a physiological match on a genetic level.

I took a deep whiff. "I don't want to sound weird, but I can *smell* you."

He looked at me, cross, his green-gray eyes were open windows.

"... I mean in a good way," I stammered. "I—just haven't smelled *anything* in months... does that make me weird?"

"Woah," he replied. "That's neat! Not the no-smelling thing, but the smell-good thing."

One of the major long-term complications of my particular brain injury is continued latent dissociation. I believe this is caused by my lack of smell. When meeting new people, because I cannot smell them, I have trouble emotionally connecting on an interpersonal level. Some sense of intimacy, gone—suffering from low libido or the desire to be physically close with people. I don't lack feelings, but lacking in connection, understanding the importance of smell is a necessity—it attracts us to others, releasing oxytocin, which forms human bonds.

As we talked, he emoted with his hands. On his palm, a rune.

"You have a rune?" I said, turning my hand to point out mine. "This means end strife. This, healing."

He widened his palm. "This one means *new life.*"

He went on to tell me that he was also hit by a car in Portland, riding his bike to work. Hit and run, out cold for days. He had no idea how he got to the hospital. It wasn't the first time either. He suffers from Chronic Traumatic Encephalopathy (CTE), a neurodegenerative disease caused by repeated blows to the head, which he often jokes is from headbanging too hard.

"You know, taking LSD is a lot like having a brain injury," he said. "The heightened senses are just indicative of extreme consciousness." A three-time veteran of concussions himself, he went on to explain the colors, feelings, and senses he had one trip after taking a sheet of LSD. "You should be proud, you're enlightened. It's called ego death."

When I was an undergrad and took a class, "The Hero." It outlined the study of attaching the ideology of literary heroes to a Jungian philosophical perspective. I painstakingly read through stories *The Divine Comedy*, *Bartleby the Scrivener*, *Rip Van Winkle*, *The Odyssey*, and James Joyce's *Ulysses*—books and cliffs notes and highlighters in hand—trying to break down the meaning of what my professor was trying to convey. And for the life of me, I could not break the mental barrier of linearity or the journey itself, the reason why these heroes would undergo such trials and tribulations for seemingly trivial things, or the fact that they'd simply resist their journey by raising the question of why.

Unlike The Hero's Journey, in which a decisive crisis wins a victory and comes home changed or transformed, ego death is a complete loss of subjective self-identity or a fundamental transformation of the psyche through psychedelics. But there was a parallel. If my brain had dissociated to protect itself and everything was stripped away except survival—working, paying bills, making appointments—I had no choice but to go through the experience of mentally mapping my way back to my current self. How did all that other stuff stick while the rest made zero sense if it wasn't the death of ego?

From across the room, I caught our reflection, Soulmate and I together, in the window.

While sitting shiva, it's Jewish tradition to cover the mirrors to encourage the inner reflection of those in mourning. This was originally based on the belief that spirits were attracted to mirrors. In their reflection, souls could be trapped to linger and may try to reach out from the other side.

This was my ego, and when it died, all that was left was my brain's will to survive. I took the journey, shed my ego, and covered the mirrors.

And in front of me—Soulmate.

Myself.

Egos dead.

From brain injuries to east coast upbringings, life, and music. From the salt and pepper in his black hair all the way down to the tattoos on his feet, I admired his intelligence and sincerity.

I felt connected. Soothed. Like I was in my body again for the very first time. I missed feeling closeness. Soulmate was a total release of oxytocin. Some neuropathologists and psychologists say that the brain does not regenerate new connections, but I wholly disagree (even in recent studies, serotonergic alternative medicines such as those in psychedelics and ketamine session-administered therapies, suggest otherwise).

Soulmate and I married two months later at a tipi in the woods.

We moved to a farm outside of Eugene, Oregon, despite my psychologist's warning of irrational behavior post-recovery.

WHOEVER YOU ARE
PART II

||||||||||||||||||||||||||||||||||||||||||||||||||||||||||||||||||||||||||||||||||||||||||||||||

FOLKS WHO SAY "you are not your job" have never been a publicist, nor perhaps lived in a city and worked such a job. Each day I woke up, before the chore of dealing with the injury, spent fifteen minutes on my face and hair, and carefully picked out an outfit that honored the weather forecast. Though I was just bustling to figure out which bus would get me to the office on time, which coffee shop I could stop at along the way, and organizing the day's tasks by in office and out of office meetings, and where I may go that evening for drinks or dinner, it was all a show. A big exhausting show.

I never stopped to think what could happen in the meantime, that I could run into an old friend, a new flame, or potentially end up in the hospital. This goes without mentioning the current emotional states, whether it'd be a hangover, a breakup, or something potentially catastrophic happening that could break open the floodgates. As they say, life is what happens when you're busy making other plans.

Still, I kept a straight face. Like the mantra in *American Beauty*, "To be successful, one must portray an image of success at all times."

Being a publicist—a professional—meant staying lateral. I never let my personal affairs or afflictions get in the way of work. I was nice and had to be nice, have character, I had to get my pitches out, and while I may have quietly grumbled and growled at small snafus or what was said in an interview or a podcast, I was still nice and got the job done. There was no room for my opinion in my work, there was no place for my identity in their work. Most of my social media accounts were private, only allowing old and new friends—not colleagues or fanboys or clients—to keep a claustrophobic distance between my work and my actual life. Mute was the word. I was all too protective of my job to even let a sliver of my own humanity appear. But in reality, it was all in my head. When push came to shove it was not me that anyone was after, it was my contact list or the catalog I was representing. At the time, I was too engrossed by it to see it. In my eyes, I was *a publicist*, I had an important job to do, so it only seemed right that I shut myself out and let the work take over.

This rang true even after my accident. I was too afraid to let anyone outside of the office know that I was in pain or couldn't get in the mindset to get the job done. I never wanted to come off as weak or incapable, so I did everything in my power to create the illusion that nothing had happened and tried to stay on the top of things, presented in a flurry of emails and social posts. I could take my time, work over an extended period to get everything right. I worked all hours, seven days a week to do it. The times I spent napping or in therapy did not take away from a job well done—I refused to allow it.

"You need a new job," my occupational therapist told me one day. "All the work is going to set back your recovery by at least a year. You need rest."

Take a break from work? *Absolutely not!* Not that my body wasn't telling me to; deep down inside I just wanted to pull the covers over my head and sleep forever. I needed support, hire a temp or take some of the workload off. Even when I called for short-term disability, I was told that it was problematic and that I would have to go for the long term. Moreover, I wouldn't necessarily qualify for long-term disability because the injury wasn't physically acquired on the job and that I could still work given the appropriate accommodations. The disability office told me that if I could watch a security camera, I could work. In hindsight it is patently obvious I needed a break but I was practically incapable of using cognitive reasoning and could barely keep my balance after something as simple as putting on a shoe. But I powered through. I had to. I simply cared too much not to.

ON ALL OF THE COVERS

IIIIIIIIIIIIIIIIIIIIIIIIIIIIIIIIIIIIIIIIIIIIIIIIIIIIIIIIIIIIIIIIIIIIIIIIIIIIIIIIIIIIIIIIIIIIIIIIIIIIIIIIIIIIIIIIIIIIIIIIIIII

"I'M A FREAK" was my mantra when I was seventeen. Self-expression on the outside and not a reflection of what inner turmoil may have been yearning on the inside. I was an ugly duckling, but age reared somewhat of a swan. Smarts only mattered after the initial hook of right hair and clothes.

Maybe that was why Kurt Cobain killed himself at the height of his career, maybe it was just a grand statement of ego death? And reading his biography at a young impressionable age, I empathized with the harrowing rags to riches story that ultimately brought him back home, gun in hand. I'm no Kurt Cobain, nor can others hold a candle, but in losing who I thought I was, it was only then that the world and my existence in it began making total sense and this was my Nirvana.

Three albums released in 1999 hit me hard: Hole's *Celebrity Skin*, Marilyn Manson's *Mechanical Animals*, and Nine Inch Nails *The Fragile*. Before that, I had Smashing Pumpkins *Mellon Collie and the Infinite Sadness*. When I picked these albums up in high school, I could never imagine the grand parallel with the decade to come. These artists are the last of the rockstars. The last of fame through talent and PR. The music industry was shifting to digital at the turn of the century, and as these musicians left the height of their careers, they angrily took to the mic to express their aggravation at what was to be the new industry norm—sanitized corporate rock in the form of auto-tune and instant download.

In October of 2018, these albums resonated their way back into my life as my frustration towards my media-driven life began to take its toll. I was a born and bred publicist, known for working rooms, taking emails, and doling out media to the press. I watched new media take off and then I watched it fade into the backdrop within weeks of it hitting the shelf. It was a contest of time and place; it was a constant content battle. With news and posts loading their way every seven seconds, onto media streams, with everyone suddenly capable of promoting unpublished or unseen works, entertainment becomes even more than ever a survival of the fittest than a practice of the heart.

When those albums were released, there were still launch parties, successful tours, and visits to largely televised awards shows. The concept of fame was still intangible; only conceived by being at the right place at the right time, having money or knowing someone with money, or being born into the business.

While talking to my analyst one day, she mentioned that her ex sold drugs to Janis Joplin, but then went on to tell me how no one was famous back then—they were just musicians playing music. So where did *fame* come from?

Soulmate, an ex-musician, suffers from post-performance depression (PPD), and static agoraphobia. He traveled all over the world. Initially, the tours and festivals were a straight-edge sober venture, which eventually moved into self-medication—unfortunate but typical for musicians living life on the road. He became an integrated, artful soul—one with nature, the earth, and himself. I learned from his ability to remain functional while concealing every ounce of discomfort he might feel by extracting himself from human contact. He thrives on consciousness and aloneness.

ONE DAY I was sitting on my porch listening to "Champagne Supernova" on a loop, I began thinking about the driver who hit me, who had been served papers just two weeks before. Denial from the insurance company transformed the accident and my injuries into a civil suit. While I felt justice was underway, I then began to think—somewhat irrationally—about the welfare of the driver and insurance company, their own emotions, as if this misstep on their part might suddenly dawn on them. And for a moment, I felt bad that I would be the cause of anyone's distress—despite what they had done to me. I'd gone over and over the rollercoaster of emotions, but from where I stood it seemed the driver hadn't. I considered that they didn't know how badly I was injured—or that their failing to pay attention, or even swerve off to avoid hitting me, ultimately resulted in the loss of the life I had been strategically building.

I went from city in Portland to farm life in Eugene, where growing gardens replaced friends, and the loss of my job left me questioning my abilities and self-worth. While being surrounded by nature grounded me, it was a hard realization that after all this time, and all the schooling and work I'd put in, I was left with the banality of starting all over again. Slowly getting my brain back, with my skull cracks now sealed and cognition returning, it was like waking up in a completely different world. I had no idea where to go and was still searching for traces of myself. With no job, I found myself with all-too-much time to think and always wanting to drink. Distractions were minimal making art, learning to tattoo, baking—what came off as productive via Instagram, was actually a way to placate the emptiness and loneliness.

The relationship with my friends back in Portland or elsewhere far, far away, devolved into meager texts. Working at least kept me sending emails and taking calls, but without it, I found myself in the waking hours watching *TGIF* reruns. With Soulmate still working and taking the car daily (which mocked my lack of willingness to step foot on the accelerator anyway) I was confined to our home in the mountains. The same isolation and anxiety I had as a kid resurfaced.

Who was I if I didn't have friends, if I didn't work, if I wasn't in the city, if I actively avoided driving and crossing streets? There was only one direction to look, and it was that of the driver who hit me. Where was this ounce of empathy I had toward them coming from?

THE OBJECT OF MY DEPRESSION

IIIIIIIIIIIIIIIIIIIIIIIIIIIIIIIIIIIIIIIIIIIIIIIIIIIIIIIIIIIIIIIIIIIIIIIIIIIIIIIIIIIIIIIIIII

EGO ASIDE, MOURNING the death of oneself is part of sustaining a brain injury. The first step is to acknowledge the injury that changed you, the self, and what is left. While I was still working, I was able to hold onto a resemblance of my former self. Despite moving away to the quiet country, work was the glue that kept me running back to Portland on occasion where I could see my friends and eat at my favorite restaurants. My office was still intact, along with my work desk as well. The knowledge and sense of accomplishment remained, but so did the clouded struggle to maintain the person I was by doing the job to the best of my ability.

And then the merger happened. Thank you, corporate America.

I lost my job at the publisher, which was a big blow.

A thread of myself that I thought was left, went away with it. (Cue the music.) *If I wasn't my job, who was I?*

This kind of grief is symptomatic and falls in line with both postconcussive syndrome as well as posttraumatic stress. It was as though I lost all my earthly belongings in a house fire or a hurricane, and survived. All that remained was the lumber, traces of paper, and broken artifacts scattered across the lawn. I also knew the person I was very well and was not sure if I could love the person I became. I may have looked and sounded like my old self, but I found it difficult and often cumbersome to make do with the person left in the wake— the changes at hand were like being confronted with a pile of rubble and given a spackle wand to build things up again.

I WAS DISCHARGED from occupational therapy in the spring. Throughout, I didn't write. I wanted to sit with myself and let the tide wash up a new perspective. Workless and focused on healing, summer simply came and went. Despite the hiring process taking place in the first and final quarters of the year, I still sought work from the comfort of my home office, which I nicknamed "Tangier." There was some excitement: I watched the vegetables planted in the garden grow, July brought the Oregon Country Fair and August held the final tour of Parliament-Funkadelic as well as a harmonious return to North Beach, and the start of September brought Melvins to Eugene.

The paralegal from my lawyer's office called to set the date in late October for deposition.

"Every time I get an email or call from the office, I start to shake," I told her.

"Yes, that's normal," she replied. "It'll all be over soon."

One night, I dreamt of sitting in a bar with all of my friends in Portland. My past loves manifested with their children, and in the dream, we said our well wishes and goodbyes, and I woke to find myself with an odd sense of ease. I don't know how this propelled me, but I grabbed the keys to the truck and for the first time drove myself into town. I ordered a breakfast of runny eggs and coffee and made a quick trip to Walmart for a few odds and ends, yet I felt something inside me shift. It was the first time I'd driven since 2017, and since the accident I had no desire to see or step foot in a car, let alone hit the gas pedal. That summer taught me that while I sat still, life trudged forward, and I had to as well, albeit little by little. I was the only one in control of my life in some ways, so if the seasons were going to change and life was going to go on, I had no choice but to move along with it. Resonating in the back of my mind was what the doctors had said, "Your recovery will happen so slowly, you won't even notice."

The pain in my ear subsided unless I was tired and then the tickle of nerve damage began to wane. I had a few moments of triggered worry and late-night paranoia over insurance company spies, lawyer emails, and thinking of the face of the person who hit me when they were served papers for the legal dispute over my case—relayed to me via email while waiting for another CT scan to check the status of the clots still in my head. There were one, two, then magically three clots. Seems each time I would have imaging done, the number changed according to the hematologist or neurologist. These clots were initially presumed to be on the opposite side of my head by another set of doctors. My disdain for the medical profession and insurance agencies grew as the bills began to surpass $58,000.

I felt very small. Because I was hit by a car, I had to go remote. Lost almost a year of life to recovery, struggled to regain my skill set, and ultimately, I wondered, if not for any of this, was it *why* I lost my job in the merger? I was flooded with remorse:

Who was I without PR?

Without my ego?

Who was I if I was no one?

Was I actually *no one*?

Will I ever be *someone*, again?

Each day I woke up in a place that I came to understand as home, but I was in a world outside of my knowledge, and in ways, my choice. I was making the best of the situation. I fed my dog, cats, goats, and chickens, and tried to create stuff—it was all I had any control over.

Along the way, perhaps it was dumb luck, but I was offered a secondary contract publicity job with a new publisher, but one that maxed out at eighteen hours a week. No guidance and complete trust as it commenced—a small step, I supposed, to make me feel a little less lost, yet not enough to financially sustain myself or my new family come the new year.

Then came fall. October. I worked hard to try and secure a full-time position in fear of unemployment benefits running out. I had four interviews, only one of which I was offered—another part-time position—with an hour commute to boot. I had no choice but to drive. On the morning of the first day of my new job, pulling out of the long driveway to meet the road, a Jeep hastily pulled around the corner as the truck I was driving touched the road. That driver, angered, lingered behind me as I obeyed the twenty miles per hour school zone only to whip around me at its end. It was early morning with fog and forked strips of sun. On the freeway, the glaring sun made it impossible to see, but I had to merge onto the proper exit. I gathered myself before walking into the building.

In uncomfortable office clothes, I walked past the gray cubicles to drop my belongings in what was dubbed "my office." Women flitted about in Kohl's blouses, gray suit pants, and those slip-on Target brand Mary Janes that I had come to associate with today's working women—simple and often wielding sores at the arc of the heel. Men were wearing polos and khakis, while fluorescent lights hung over them with a distilling presence. Though uncomfortable and unfamiliar, I was determined to put my best foot forward and try. So, I did. Trying my best to use my brain to be kind and maneuver through solving the puzzles of each task expected of me. It wasn't PR.

It wasn't familiar. None of it made much sense outside of a simple part-time dollar figure.

The next day came, I was off. It was a Friday. Working my other PR job remotely, I was standing out by the barn with my chickens. An email came from my ex-husband, who I had not spoken to since he brought a box of my favorite chocolates to my apartment weeks after the accident. The email said that he and his girlfriend had been hit dead-on by another car on the 101. I sat with a quiet sadness and conferred with friends in Seattle who had insisted on taking him what he needed.

Monday came. At 3:30 in the morning, Soulmate was asleep on the couch and I woke in bed with an augmented pang of anxiety. I shook and I waited for it to subside.

It didn't. Something wasn't right.

I tried to dismiss the fear, but couldn't, thinking about getting in the car and driving; thinking about the man who angrily jetted past me just a few days before the merger, and my ex. I was flooded with thoughts of car accidents and those I knew who were in them; it was all too many. Trying to shut that part of my brain off, I turned on the latest audiobook by Patti Smith, *The Year of the Monkey*, to coincide with the low hum of the sleep sound machine above the bed. I struggled in my pajama cocoon until the morning traffic and logging trucks whizzing down the road rendered me sleepless. When my alarm went off at 6:30 AM, I surrendered to the daylight and went downstairs.

"I'm not going to work," I said to Soulmate. "I can't—not now, not ever."

Dazed in a half-slumber, he moved cats and the dog as he sloughed the blankets off to sit up. "It's okay," he said, perhaps knowing what was going through my mind.

We made pity pancakes and coffee while simultaneously drafting an email to the employer on my phone. In the end, my employer agreed that I would complete some of the work remotely to be seen out over the next few weeks. Throughout that week all I could think about were cars—cars hitting people.

The deposition was weeks away. With all that had happened within a single week, I couldn't help but wonder if I was in the wrong mind, or the right one; the natural one, the PTSD one. I wanted to claw my skin off, ink myself to the nines, liquidate my bank account and run off and live in a tent on the street like a train-hopping hobo. I wanted to run off to Scotland, Iceland, live in one set of clothes, and fade off into oblivion. My head was swimming with fear and with questions, nothing on the outside mattered and I truly felt as if nothing would or could save me at all.

THIRD EVERYTHING

|||||||||||||||||||||||||||||||||||||||||||||||||||||||||||||||||||||||||||||||||||||||||||

HOTEL DELUXE. PORTLAND, OR, October 29th, 2019:

I'll admit that never in my life had I thought about suicide. It's the day before my deposition, the day I've been dreading having to defend my life since the accident itself.

I got to Portland around 2PM—only to learn that they moved the BOLT stop to the east side of the city. My hotel, on the southwest side. Crossing no streets, I got on the MAX train as I had a million times before. I stopped at Sephora to get the chemical peel wipes I like, took out a large sum of cash at the ATM, and tried on clothing that I couldn't afford, but purchased a pair of jeans I didn't need anyway.

I'm at the hotel bar, eating a carrot salad, trying to draft a press release. There's a cupcake waiting for me in my room—the "Big Top" yellow cake with fudge frosting. I'll put the carrot salad on the room. I can't afford this swanky hotel, but it doesn't matter, I wholly intend that this is the last place I'll stay.

The bourbon isn't working. The exhaustion is real. I'm thinking about my past self—now I feel feeble, feeling elderly, nodding off in this dimly lit room. There is a couple next to me celebrating their anniversary. The man brought roses and two cards to his significant other. They are eating mac and cheese, talking about their workday. There are four men across from them, attorneys, which I wouldn't have noticed until one of them mentioned Joe Walsh.

I'm writing this here because this is my last sacred letter. I've been muted from the lawsuit and my ever-standing career as a publicist. I can't tell anyone. Not my Soulmate, my friends, or family what I'm feeling—not even my therapist who would undoubtedly "push the red button" if made aware of my current mental state.

This is the most depressed I've ever been in my whole life. If suicidal is this, then I'm it. I've never been here before, but mentally, it feels like rock bottom. Why—not, Why Me? I made choices to move forward against all odds, I've succeeded—even once lamenting "As long as no one gets in my head, I'll be fine." Well. That's happened. I don't know who I am anymore. I'm too tired and weak to think or believe that anything, that happiness is possible, anymore. I've lived my best life in my past life, now here I am; third life, third everything, and I am not equipped. I won't ever win. That light I had has faded.

So I'm here, at Hotel Deluxe, the hotel I've longed to stay in for over a decade. I'm here because recently I've thought too many times about not existing—not the act of suicide, but simply "being" no longer. It's hard not knowing who you are when you've worked all your life to be somebody. I hardly matter to anyone, let alone myself, and who's that? My life, even in dollar figures according to the state and the legal system, isn't even worth my student loan debt. I've lost touch with everything—my "friends" my "family" my "home." I'm so far away from anything and everything, so what's there to defend? I'll admit that before all this I was shallow, all I cared about was knowing the right people and having a nice purse, and I hate that person. I love and hate that person. I did it all wrong. I thought I was alive and have to talk myself off this ledge. I have nothing left to lose.

Fuck you, person who hit me. Fuck everything.

I liked my facade, it was safe.

HAPPINESS IS A VIRTUE, BUT IT'S A LONG UPHILL BATTLE TO GET IT, THEN KEEP IT.

I'M DONE.

YOU TOOK IT ALL. YOU WON.

XO, Melissa

ABOVE—WRITTEN WITH THE deposition and the defense exam dates looming. The next day, I was placed in a room with two legal professionals and a stenographer, in front of a tape recorder, having to hold my composure. All the while, knowing full well that both my lawyer and the insurance company attorney were casually discussing baseball stats before pressing the record button and settling down with their notebooks.

It was difficult to concentrate with the sounds of cars and trains and trucks pumping against the windows. I was tired from travel.

The flattened emerald carpet and the mahogany decor were all too reminiscent of a funeral home; the words of a funeral director came to me: "There won't be much left by way of ashes, your daughter was very small at the time of her death."

The defense attorney wore a gray fleece quarter-zip, was bald and not at all intimidating as we ran through the exact same questions that I'd been asked a million times over throughout the course of the case.

"Were you on your phone?"

"No," I replied. "My phone was in my pocket. The last text message I sent was in the foyer of the building."

My lawyer checked her records. "Yes, shortly after five-thirty. The accident occurred several minutes later."

The defense took note. Paused. "This happened around the time of the anniversary of your daughter's death. You had just gotten divorced. Were you feeling depressed?"

I curled my thumb into my sweater, which was shaking in my lap. "No, I was on my way to see Judas Priest."

He chortled. "I know you go to a lot of concerts. I saw your post about the Melvins."

I shook my head, thinking about the screenshots I had to provide as evidence before setting my profiles to private. It was very hard to stop myself from reeling in anger but I was coached beforehand to say yes or no, along with brief answers.

The process took three hours. They dug into my past, my relationships, where I lived and what schools I went to—*and why and how and what did it all mean?* How was the story of my entire life relevant to what took less than ten seconds to occur, all because some inattentive numbnut impatiently drove a car and struck me?

In my closing statement, agitated, I firmly claimed, "I was in a very good place before this. I lost my brain, my health, and my job. *Your client* took that all away from me"

The defense took a deep breath, his eyes glassy, perhaps almost showing remorse. I took pity on his position, realizing he was just a cog in the system. This was not humanity; it was a paycheck. In light of this, my thoughts of simply "not existing" began to retract.

As I went to put my coat on, my lawyer confirmed the time of the defense exam. She told me most likely they would give me a physical, check how well I can balance standing on each foot, and that it should only take an hour.

I WOKE EARLY the morning of the defense exam, donned my Sunday best, and told myself that the quicker I got through it, the quicker I could GTFO there for a spaghetti lunch.

Not so much.

My lawyer warned me that the doctor was vicious, a real wolf in sheep's clothing. She even had a nickname to reflect her nature.

They sat me in a dark room. The nurse asked, "What do you want for lunch?"

"What do you mean?" I asked, somehow maintaining politeness.

"This takes all day. I'll order you a bagel." And shut the door.

It was oddly warm in there, moist almost. There were two lamps adjacent to the table. Only two chairs.

The doctor came in and sat down. Gaunt, ghostlike, with wavy shoulder-length hair.

Softly, she asked, "How are you today?"

"As good as can be expected."

Questions, questions. It was like taking the DMV exam with the most repetitive questions.

No, for the last time, I was not suicidal because my baby died a decade ago. Why were they so obsessed with this?! Was it the only leg they had to stand on? Please, explain to me how someone so successful and independent would be so bummed during pizza week.

The doctor took the last of her notes and another woman entered the room, hauling a wagon and briefcase. She laid a series of blocks on the table—all primary colors, all different shapes.

"Replicate this."

From blocks to memory lists to identifying pictures, my delay in processing was pretty apparent to me.

I took a deep breath and put my hands flat on the table. "It's an a-a-ahhh-bacus? Abacus?"

"Are you asking me?" the woman fumed.

"This is too much," I said. My hands started to tremble. My head started to twitch. "I can't—I can't do this anymore. This is too much."

She crossed her arms. "We have *four* more hours."

"I want to speak to my lawyer."

I grabbed my phone. She showed me the door. I was warned there were cameras planted everywhere in the office.

MEDIATION CAME. ME and my lawyer, the defense, and a retired judge convened to discuss what might be a mutually beneficial resolution to the case. This is an experience that no one should endure. The figure, my lawyer and I surmised, was nowhere near what the defense had returned with. Flat out they said, "There's no six-figure number."

This is a bidding war, waged by corporate adjusters and the insurer's lawyer. The defendant, the man who hit me, was not inconvenienced in the slightest by having to be present. But back to the lack of a six-figure figure. Despite the physical damage, recovery, economic loss, and emotional distress, to the insurance companies we are all simply a statistic! Remember that whole thing about net worth? Yeah, well, even primed and prim in a suit from Ann Taylor, as it was, while the defendant moved on about his life with no real understanding or even apparent apology given the situation of nearly killing me, my net worth, according to the insurance adjuster was worth a third of less than a six-figure number. To put this in further perspective, perched on a mahogany chair in my Lawyer's office, both she and the judge's jaws simply dropped. The scream. The acid trip drips melting faces away from the bone. My medical bills alone had bumped up to a final whopping $85k, I have permanent brain damage and vertigo because stimuli of general living, noise, movement, little smell, and libido, put my head into a shameful spin so completely vomit-inducing, that I may as well have never left home.

So why so little? They threatened to hold me fifty percent responsible, if not more, for "failing to maintain proper lookout" in court. If I hadn't maintained proper lookout—*ahem*—how would I have safely crossed the other lanes of traffic? Brass tacks—a person in all impatience, zipped around another car and whacked me.

But it gets worse...

It's estimated that ninety-five percent of all cases settle out of court, which made me wonder if all lawyers bare a false sense of compassion to enhance their own net worth without the headache of having to approaching the bench.

The highly revered mediation judge said, "Think of it like this: You have tattoos, you were on your way to a concert to see a metal band. They are a successful upper-class businessperson who was most likely on their way home to take their kids to soccer." She paused to gather herself. "Your fate lies within a jury. Twelve people who don't know you, but decide right or wrong based on their own opinions and beliefs, not necessarily facts. That decision could land you winning the full amount, considering you partially at fault with 50%, or leaving you not only with nothing but having to pay court costs, which are 10k a day. If you don't pay it, you could go to jail."

If I heard correctly, not only did I get knocked out and racked up a shit-ton of unnecessary medical debt, but I also lost my job. And with every intention to fight for my rights, I could lose and potentially go to jail? As Amanda Knox said to Alec Baldwin on his radio show *Here's the Thing*—Everyone should have to take civics!

I picked up the pathetic wad of cash and myself by the bootstraps. A once-considered suicide mission would only let *them* win.

This was bigger than me. *THIS*—was some serious bullshit.

YOU CAN NEVER GO HOME AGAIN

I FLIPPED ON The Gits, dyed my hair red, and took a trip east. If I really was nothing after trying so hard to become something, life's delusion sent me back to Pennsylvania, my childhood home, in search of reason.

In PA, greeted by the comfort of a thunderstorm, I rolled out of the airport and into the first joint I could find. Pita bread and wing sauce with a side salad chased with a pint of Yuengling. A friend from high school met me for more beer at our favorite punk dive. I dropped dollars to hear some Motörhead and then we caught up. He'd just become an uncle and in the same week had a friend overdose.

Curled up in the red vinyl booth, he sat across from me, poking at a basket of fries. "My brother had a TBI," his scraggly beard muttered under a foreboding expression. "He got it while playing ding dong ditch. Showed up back at the house with a chipped tooth and in a state of delirium. You should also meet another friend of mine who was hit by a car seven years ago. She's fine. Even has a Ph.D."

Days later, in that very same booth, I sat there with another friend who informed me had lost her child seven months into her pregnancy, just as I had.

"I'll never be the same," she admitted, somber, fidgeting with her hands. Her eyes glazed as if it happened yesterday and not years before.

I wasn't special or different. Pain is objective; experiences, similar.

There's nothing about my getting hit by a car, sustaining a brain injury, or even losing a baby that made my pain of the experience any lesser or greater than anyone else's. There was nothing about where I lived or who I knew or what I did or even lived through that set me apart as anything but human.

THE FOLLOWING DAY, I rented a car and drove the hour north to my childhood neighborhood and to visit my grandparent's gravesite. Not a Smurf or Jabberwocky in sight, as my childhood imagination had once conjured—just a row of houses that looked as exactly as I left them. I named off each family as I passed by, making the trek down to the old park on the next block. It gave me a warm feeling that the swing set remained, but they had updated the slides and put in a small communal library.

I arrived at the cemetery and was the only one present, save a groundskeeper. The sky was ripped by strips of cirrus clouds. The grass pricked my hands. As I talked to my grandparents headstone, tears of joy—not sadness—fell down my cheeks. Eating through a box of assorted chocolates picked up along the way, I audibly consulted over where I should get a spaghetti dinner. I gifted a wreath of lilacs to my grandmother and played Johnny Cash for my grandfather. I said nothing of the accident, my injury, my sadness or lostness, nothing of the difficulties of the past few years. Coming back home in cut-off shorts and combat boots, flannel tied around my waist, sitting next to my grandparents, a familiar feeling came over me.

I took a breath and said, "It will happen so slowly, that you won't even notice."

My mind suddenly flipped to the notion of fame, of being famous, of how people view fame and how people acquire fame. Is it drive, circumstance, or sheer luck—perhaps a little of each? Back in the era of vaudeville, well into the talkies, folks had to have talent. You had to be able to act, sing, and dance if you were going to make it to the silver screen.

A few famous people made it out of my hometown, namely Trent Reznor, who I came to know as my high school algebra teacher's relative and the art teacher's nemesis. He used to play the venue where we all slung chicken wings in our teens and twenties, which at that time was called Seafood Express. I also heard rumors that Patrick Swayze hung out there while in town filming *Tiger Warsaw*.

Ed O'Neill of the hit '90s show, *Married with Children*, was a local thespian and athlete who frequented The Wave Italian restaurant. Gameshow host Alex Trebek stayed at the country inn less than a mile from my childhood home.

Stiv Bators from The Dead Boys grew up just a half-hour away. He died in his sleep as the result of a traumatic brain injury after being hit by a car in Paris.

IN THE MID-1800S, circus clown and entertainer Dan Rice was a household name. The winter home for his circus was just over an hour north of where I grew up. He originated the term "Greatest Show on Earth" and won the affection of many publicists and newspapers, including the likes of Mark Twain and Walt Whitman. A man of many talents, Rice began as a clown, working his way up to producing shows. He was the first to combine animals, acrobats, and clowns in the circus. He did vaudeville before there was vaudeville. He set fashion trends, wrote songs, and parodied current affairs and literary classics. Campaigning for twelfth President Zachary Taylor, he coined the phrase "Jump on the Bandwagon." He would later run for President.

Even his biographer called him 'the most famous person you've never heard of.'

Maybe he needed a better publicist.

THE QUESTION REMAINED: *What exactly was I running from all this time?* What I can recall of living in Pennsylvania in my late teens to my early twenties doesn't seem all bad in retrospect. I had friends, I had a car, I had a job. Sometimes I like to think if the internet was as dependable as it is today, I never would've left. Granted there are always life's peaks and valleys, but nothing was ever so horrible that I actually had to go. But go I did. "The unexamined life is not worth living," or so they say. Realizing one's "full potential"—I absolutely hated the word *potential*. To me, it devalued my very existence. Why have potential when you can have experience and knowledge? I took a risk and lived quite a few lives in between then and now, but when push came to shove, I'm still the exact same person in some ways (or so I think). I have the values of an altruist, I don't like friction, I still enjoy baggy t-shirts and jeans with a perfect patina, I still like the same music and foods. But my potential, my perspective, I continually question. *Who am I? Who was I trying to be?*

I can honestly say that if I wasn't able to look back and know that I tried to be anyone at all, I would've disappointed no one but myself. No one ever set up expectations for me, I always marched to the beat of my own drum. I try to be a good person, unselfish and kind and can recognize those who aren't. Whoever you are, no matter what, life has value. It's up to us to treat life as a journey and not a destination.

WITH ALL THE fuckery I had to endure between corporate entities, the law, and the medical field, it was time to take it from the man in the best way I knew how: to be my own entity who supports indie creators, the underdogs, and dreamers.

Don't Hide PR launched in 2019—that's my comics PR company. The question stood: why entertainment and why comics after sustaining a traumatic brain injury? It was the ONLY thing that wasn't knocked out of me. Like connection to an AA program, the community that comics gave me, activated my parasympathetic nervous system. Kind nerds creating—I began to understand that deep down, I was one of them. And I wanted to create in my own way—through fighting for creators outside of a system.

I had the tools, the experience and the network contacts, so why couldn't I set out to do PR on my own? Sure as shit, I wasn't going to let a "damaged brain" stand in the way. If that car knocked a few screws loose, I was convinced it was the bad ones. I had risen from a darker ash and came out as my true self. I'm no martyr, but I always champion those with a good heart and deep passion to create, or even recreate. I liked the idea of helping people find the audience to share their work with.

Key words: Don't Hide. It's the least we can do. Raise your Black Flag and hope for the best.

AFTERWORD

IIIIIIIIIIIIIIIIIIIIIIIIIIIIIIIIIIIIIIIIIIIIIIIIIIIIIIIIIIIIIIII

FOR A MOMENT, I accepted everything. Things were actually almost good. Don't get me wrong—I hold onto every moment as if it were the last because the one thing I've learned is that life if fleeting.

Soulmate and I moved away from the farm onto the river bend, deep in the Willamette Forest, the million-dollar neighborhood was worth the view we could barely afford. Once the 5G router was installed, I headed up to Portland to sign the paperwork to close the case on the car accident. Upon arriving home, I took a deep breath and said, "Finally, life is ahead of me." Spending so much time rehashing the past, paying my dues, and tying up loose ends of all that was before the moment, it *finally* felt like a done deal.

THEN THERE WAS the fire.

The power went out early that night while I was waxing my legs in the living room, boxes still packed. Lights out.

Soulmate and I turned on my iPad that had a few rogue episodes of *LA Ink* downloaded before heading off to bed. Winds were gusting outside, but it was nothing that we weren't used to, living in the

Oregon valley. A power line down, no big deal—off to the coffee shop the next morning to work if the power wasn't restored.

Morning came. 6am and still dark, odd for early September. I headed towards the bathroom, feeling my way around the chimney in the center of the house. Upon further inspection, the sky, the forest was glowing. Red. Not just the burgeoning orange of a morning sky—it was the firelight of *Apocolypse Now*. I walked to the edge of the sliding door towards the deck and felt a deep fear. The pit of my stomach wrenched as it did the morning I'd lost my daughter. Death loomed in a new and mysterious way. Sirens wailed from far off.

"Babe?? Come here?" I said aloud from the living room, knowing Soulmate was still in bed, fast asleep.

In a darkened slumber, he stirred and pulled himself out of bed.

"This doesn't feel right," I said. "We need to go."

Cat food. Dog food. Pet crates. With my work bag and travel case, we huried through the dark. When we opened the front door, smoke plumed though, even though a fire was nowhere in sight.

How inconvenient. I had to work today.

I watched a police officer pull up to the gate. "HEY! Get out NOW!" he yelled.

"Thanks for the warning!" I shouted, pulling the truck door closed.

As we pulled away, a parade of vehicles trailed the police around trees that were downed by the winds. I sat in the passenger's seat, hugging my cat.

"It's okay," I told her. "We'll be home later."

I was emotionally prepared. I'd gone down this path already.

ON THE MORNING back in 2018, hours before I was hit by the car, I thought I was at the pinnacle of my career. I had control of my life. I had my career. I was living in the city I loved and called home, I had a very nice apartment, wonderful friends, and I thought that the search for myself was over. Objects in the rearview mirror may appear closer than they seem.

In *The Year of Magical Thinking*, Joan Didion uses the expression "the ordinary." The mornings of Pearl Harbor and 9/11 are, she says, ordinary; that everything before a calamity seems ordinary. I remember my own morning, exchanging text messages that warmed my heart, having to update my passport to go to Canada the following month, and filing for an extension on my taxes. I wasn't plagued, I was simply looking forward to eating pizza and seeing Judas Priest— my own personal version of *Heavy Metal Parking Lot*—as the sun rose beyond the bridges of Portland, the light so warmingly refracting off the ridges of the Willamette River. What would've been a legendary day for one reason, became legendary for another.

When I lost the baby, I became fixated on the narrative of before and after, that when a catastrophe happens, who we once were no longer holds merit in who we become. We can look back, evaluate and reevaluate. But what happens when we have become the person we had always wanted to be, and where do you go from there when it's taken from you? It wasn't my choice to have all that I worked so hard for, from being a waitress to a student, teacher, and entertainment publicist, taken away from me. *But had it?*

Before and after is an ever-evolving concept. Even with a brain injury, by setting myself back by months and years to prove my worth, I just kept going. I had to. It was all I knew. Despite disassociation, my knowledge and drive of what I knew had to be done, remain with me beyond anything else. So this was ordinary, so to speak. My ordinary. But when life changes in an instant, fight or flight kicks in. And then ultimate emotional draining that left me in the dark. This pain would resurface again and again, manifesting itself in all-new ways when catastrophe struck.

There was a quote I held onto as a teenager: "We must keep working, finding a dream to run towards. A life without dreaming is simply too impossible to imagine." I can't remember if it was Sylvia Plath or Emily Dickinson who originally said it, but my agilely rewiring brain tells me that it was pulled from either the Frances Farmer autobiography or Deborah Spungen's biography of Nancy Spungen, *And I Don't Want to Live This Life: A Mother's Story of Her Daughter's Murder.*

I started dreaming again—almost lucidly and nightly. Locked in my own reality away from everything, my brain created these 'scapes of television, music, shows, celebrity, and real life. One night, I dreamt about Crush, who had enrolled in culinary school. It was during a gala that I poked my head into a room where he stood, a normal graying haircut styled as if he just walked out of a Great Clips, wearing a tan apron that simply read "culinary school." Even in my dream, I felt the palpable deflation of my adoration. He turned and asked the question, "Did you just love me for my status?"

I ask myself what truths are just beneath the surface. Had I spent my entire life vying for the closeness of celebrity for my own personal gain, or did I really care about others' success?

Answer: People are people. Famous or not.

Being a good human, nurturing others' creativity and passion is what I do.

I'm not in the business of "famous." Not now, not ever again.

We can all dream because the avoidance of dreams is not an option, at least not for me. Dreaming is a question of happiness and fulfillment. With each mapped out and even uncharted circumstance, there has to be a dream unfurling. All things must pass. And maybe I predicated too much on the past and the objectives of others to find my own objectives. That I used other people's opinions and trajectories of who I was to become, who I was, or hoped to be. It was not now and I am not before. Life will never be what it was, neither will I.

ORIGINAL TRUE-LIFE STORIES & MEMOIR

OILONWATERPRESS.COM